MEN

DON'T TALK ABOUT ...

Cancer of the Prostate and Depression

IAN NEWBEGIN, PHD

Men Don't Talk About ...

MEN

DON'T TALK ABOUT ...

Cancer of the Prostate and Depression

IAN NEWBEGIN

BALBOA.
PRESS
A DIVISION OF HAY HOUSE

Balboa Press books may be ordered through booksellers or by contacting:

Balboa Press
A Division of Hay House
1663 Liberty Drive
Bloomington, IN 47403
www.balboapress.com.au
1-(877) 407-4847

Because of the dynamic nature of the Internet, any web addresses or links contained in this book may have changed since publication and may no longer be valid. The views expressed in this work are solely those of the author and do not necessarily reflect the views of the publisher, and the publisher hereby disclaims any responsibility for them.

The author of this book does not dispense medical advice or prescribe the use of any technique as a form of treatment for physical, emotional, or medical problems without the advice of a physician, either directly or indirectly. The intent of the author is only to offer information of a general nature to help you in your quest for emotional and spiritual well-being. In the event you use any of the information in this book for yourself, which is your constitutional right, the author and the publisher assume no responsibility for your actions.

Printed in the United States of America.

ISBN: 978-1-4525-0267-0 (sc)
ISBN: 978-1-4525-0268-7 (e)

Balboa Press rev. date: 10/25/2011

To my family, especially my wife, for her patience.

Contents

Introduction

The prostate is about the same size as a walnut, but where the walnut is tough and hard, the prostate is soft and spongy. So, if you are about to have surgery on your prostate, the amount of material removed is minimal and can be performed with keyhole surgery.

This book is written for males who want to understand what cancer of the prostate means in relatively simple terms because they suspect that they have, or have been diagnosed as having, the disease. The psychological disease depression is also included as a separate discussion since many men will not talk about it either, and it has been shown that cancer of the prostate and depression often go hand in hand. There is a need to *demystify* both of these diseases since too many men fear what can often be a relatively quick fix.

The information provided is based on my personal experience with the diseases cancer of the prostate and depression. The experiences and emotions are real, and the book is my attempt to provide you, the reader, with an empathy for my position so that you can gain a better understanding of what may happen to you in the future, should you need a check on your prostate or, indeed, have some procedure performed.

I undertook additional research to provide you with a nonclinical view of the various processes which may be performed, along with a description of the disease.

Personal advice is given to help you through the process should you need to proceed further. The best advice that can be given from the outset is: *listen to and take guidance from your doctor.*

All technical information is accurate as far as I have ascertained, only the language and formatting has been modified for simplicity.

I sincerely hope that this material will be of benefit to you. Although I have briefly described the disease and its treatment, you should make the decision about which path you should take *in consultation with your doctor,* not based on the material presented in this book. I therefore bear no responsibility for decisions made by you regarding any procedure involving the prostate.

What follows is written in chronological order so that you can get a feel for what may lie ahead for yourself or your loved one, and to assure you that you are, indeed, in the safe hands of your doctor. I spoke openly with my doctors, and they freely gave information about my condition. The doctors worked constantly to assure me that I had a very good chance of surviving the disease, long into old age, and you know what? I believe them.

I understand that a significant number of males don't like visiting doctors for any reason. I am also aware that many males ignore symptoms, or with the help of a mate, explain the symptom away, often laughingly and to the detriment of their health.

Nobody likes to think that they may be ill, particularly when there are no ill effects in the first place! I was ignorant of my fate because I didn't feel ill. I also thought that there wasn't any need to visit my local doctor. The consequences could have been dire. *Cancer* is a chronic illness, and more often than one would like, *depression* follows.

As for depression, I suffered the malady for years, feeling miserable and making my family suffer from something that I could have fixed *if only I had spoken up.* Ah, but I didn't want anyone to know how I felt. My feelings were private, and after all, what can anyone do about it? Believe me; a lot can be done to relieve the debilitating feelings that go with depression.

Many males consider it *unmanly* to have depression, so they hide it. Bravado is the path to take when one wants to delude one's friends and family. Something can be done about it. Depression is not a disorder to fear or to hide. Many men suffer this insidious disease alone when there is no need.

In general, men *detest* going to see a doctor, for any reason. Men avoid seeing a medical practitioner for fear of the consequences, yet strangely enough, the consequences are what will keep them in good health. Imagine for the moment that you have cancer, but you don't know it—yet. Imagine that you *suspect* having cancer; do you want to know? If you don't go to a doctor, it may be too late and the usual consequence for *late* diagnosis is death. But, if you go to your doctor, even though you may feel anxious about what might be said, your chances of survival increase significantly. Ignorance is not bliss; it's just ignorance.

Early Thinking

A Child's View of Disease

Our perception of what can simply be called *disease* begins at childhood, and if the child's *perception* is *incorrect,* it can prevent us from taking the appropriate corrective action later in life and all because of a long-held, misguided belief. Consider the following scenario.

Way back in the fifties when I was a young child in grade five, a boy was hit by a cricket ball on the knee whilst fielding the ball. By the end of the year, the young lad was dead—from cancer. Whether or not the ball incident caused the growth of cancer is beside the point. Being young, most of the students at the school associated the hit on the knee by the ball with the cancer, and we were all very careful how we chased or gathered a ball in the future. I was affected so much by this incident that I avoided playing cricket, particularly if a hard ball was used. It was indeed a strange belief, but after all, the boy was ill after the incident and later died.

Many adults believe that a hit on the body (the location changes with the individual) can cause cancer. There is no evidence to support this odd belief, but nevertheless I, like my unknown allies, held on to the myth *just in case.*

Again, when I was young, I had developed a strange image of what cancer looked like. I had never heard of the disease, except that a fellow student had died from it. This gave me free rein to use my imagination to gain a specific belief about the disease. For me, cancer was an invasive disease which spread like a spider web throughout the body. Its colour was black, and I imagined a black web-like substance spreading throughout the body. Was there any pain? I don't know! I knew very little about cancer other than the fact that it could spread throughout the body and, more often than not, resulted in death. I had never known anyone with cancer, nor had my friends known anyone with the disease other than the child at school; however, we students weren't privy to any information about the boy's health prior to his death, other than the fact that he died from cancer, and this we attributed to the hit on the knee.

A childhood friend of mine had a strong fear of dying from cancer well into adulthood. He believed that cancer caused the body to melt away to nothing, leaving a living mass which needed constant care. I can't imagine what he saw in his mind's eye; he hadn't seen anyone with cancer during his childhood, though he also knew of the young lad who had been hit with the cricket ball. Though I don't know what his belief is today—we lost contact with each other—I daresay it has been corrected, but I bet his fear would still be based on old images of the disease.

An unfortunate fact about the child's death is that I can't remember his name, nor can I remember what he looked like. He was soon forgotten by the school population, but we did not forget the incident. Hard knocks can cause cancer, or so I believed.

What was your childhood belief about cancer? Was it as fanciful as my belief or that of my friend? Does it affect the way you think about cancer today?

When we were young, nothing seemed to worry us. We took risks and held dearly to the belief "it won't happen to me." How many "bronzed" bodies do you see during summertime? How often is it reported that skin cancer is a leading cause of death for people of *all* ages? Yet, many people continue to take risks through long exposure to the sun or under a UV light so that they get the perfect suntan. Obviously, the perfect tan can only be achieved if we sit in the sun or lie near naked under a solarium. There's no risk, right? Well, is there? Do I hear, "Nah, it won't happen to me"?

Here's another strange belief from my childhood. I remember when I had my tonsils removed as a young child. I was excited about going to the children's hospital, and after the procedure, I lay in bed feeling sore and sorry for myself. Before the operation, there was a bed at the head of the ward with a sick child in it. I thought that he was "king of the kids" because of the position of his bed, which looked down the ward. After I woke from the horrible chloroform (thank God for the new anaesthetics) and looked over at the bed, it was empty. I thought the boy had died! When my mother came to take me home, I was morbid. Mum had to get a nurse to explain to me that the boy had been allowed to go home. Again, how many kids develop strange beliefs about hospitals and disease? It's important to sit with your child to give him or her reassurance and to answer questions about his or her belief. Hospitals are not places of death; many lives are saved in a hospital, so why commit to this fear? Why let your child *fear* such institutions?

Visit a children's hospital and study the number of kids dying from cancer. These children neither asked to get cancer nor deserved to get it, but the hand of fate works in mean ways. Imagine how you would feel if a child of yours had cancer! You'd be very upset, of that I have no doubt. How would you feel seeing your child suffering from chemotherapy, losing his or her hair, and suffering the pain of the procedure? You'd put on a brave face and treasure every moment with your child, wouldn't you?

What about yourself? Do you harbour an irrational belief about cancer? Does it involve a shortening of your life? Do you hold a morbid image of yourself dying in hospital?

Doesn't your family deserve to have you around for a long time? If you are the person suffering from an illness, whether cancer or not, it doesn't matter, and if the illness is life threatening, how would your family feel seeing you in hospital? Would you continue to put on a brave face?

I know I'm asking a lot of questions and am not answering them, but I hope that you are. Understand what I am saying and what I am asking. Don't pay lip-service to what is written in this document. *You are loved by your family*, and they *deserve* to be able to support you.

Every day we take risks in life and in our jobs. The risks may be small, but risk we do. Without risk, our choices are limited and opportunities may be missed, but why do most males take risks with their health by *avoiding* a medical check? Could it be related to the risks we take in life and that we *fear* the possible *consequence*—failure—or is it simply the macho thing to do to not have a medical evaluation? Don't you owe it to your family to have a medical checkup? After all, an early health inspection may alleviate the picture painted above where your family is sitting around your deathbed.

I don't know the statistics, but I am certain that many deaths because of cancer could have been averted *if a medical health check had been performed* earlier than the original diagnosis of the cancer.

"Nah! What for? I'm as healthy as an ox. I don't need to see a doctor." Unfortunately for many men, these are famous last words: "It won't happen to me."

I was full of bravado. I never thought that I would suffer from cancer. *Neither did my brother and my cousin,* yet *we all* have undergone a radical prostatectomy. Life goes on. The story unfolds below.

Cancer Touches Everyone

Before I had my prostate removed, my experience with cancer was gained through the kids at school. I am, or was, a teacher. One of my students died from leukaemia, which had an enormous effect on all the students in that grade level. The students were devastated about losing one of their friends, but they endured the ordeal and are now getting on with their lives.

This was also the year that I found out about my own cancer, but the students didn't know this fact. What was evident to me was the impact cancer had on the students. They worked tirelessly that year to raise money for cancer research, a factor that made me and the staff very proud.

Another source of my experience with cancer was through some of the students' parents who contracted cancer, though thankfully, they were very few. A student who is directly affected by his or her parent's fate is devastated, obviously. It affects the student's friends and the staff, particularly more so when the parent was active within the school community. But, hey, *it wasn't me.* I'm okay, and nothing will happen to me. Have you ever had thoughts like this? Again, famous last words for those who ignore the symptoms.

My sister had cancer of the womb after she had four children, but happily, she is cancer-free *after thirty years*. The disease *can be defeated*. My sister has never looked back since she had her operation and subsequent radiation treatment and looks like she will live well into old age. Think about it—there were *four* people in my family who had cancer.

It's likely that we all know someone with the dreaded disease and can sympathise with them. After all, *"It isn't me,"* right? I used to think like this, and I dare say millions of people worldwide think the same way. *Cancer can touch anyone*, even you or a member of your family. There is no special immunity because of status or money. I don't want to sound heartless by using the phrase, *"It isn't me,"* but unfortunately, many people think that way.

I am retired now, but at my previous place of employment, a secondary school, I had the privilege of being a year-eight homeroom teacher, and during a class discussion, we hit on the topic of cancer because one of the students had an uncle who had cancer of the prostate. Since I had suffered from this disease, I became curious and asked the class if anyone else knew someone who had *this* disease. Four more students said they had an uncle or a grandparent with cancer of the prostate, so I asked the students if they knew anyone with cancer. *Every hand went up*. We have come a long way since I was a child, or is the term cancer vocalised more?

When I asked them if they knew someone who had died from cancer, about half the number of hands went up.

Think about that! *Every student* knew someone with cancer, and 50 percent of the students experienced the *trauma* of a loved one or close friend dying from this insidious disease.

Anyway, back to my class. We talked about cancer for a little while, and it became apparent that the students were really sensitive towards the disease and were quite knowledgeable about it. When I told them about this book, some of the students said that they'd like to write something about their own experience, so I asked them if they'd allow me to include their work here.

I am sure you will be touched by the students' expression of their feelings. If you think that nobody is touched by cancer, read on. All stories are in their original form.

Shannon writes:

> My name is Shannon, and I have lost three people and one pet to cancer. I lost one of my pet dogs, Mindy, who I was really close to. I lost my grandpa about five years ago. I was close to him and felt his death. I also lost both of my nanas, and because of this, I never got to meet them, so I never had a grandma, only a step-nana.
>
> At the time of Mindy's death, my sister and I were too young, but it still affected us. But when my grandpa died, it was really hard on the family, especially my mum because she had lost her mum to cancer and now her dad. An effect all this had on me has been that for the past five years, I have only had one grandparent. This one grandparent is my poppy on my dad's side. Some days I feel really low and miss them very much, but I always know they are looking down on me and watching over me.
>
> For a short time, my whole family was down, but we always made it though. Sometimes I feel like I have missed out on things like talking to my grandma or having Christmas with Grandpa.

Kate writes:

> Last year in 2006, a good friend of ours got diagnosed with breast cancer. When we found out, I was scared for her, hoping she would pull through like last time. K (name withheld) was a wonderful person who lived life to the fullest. It's just sad that cancer took that away from her. As the days went on, K eventually got worse, worse enough that she had to be taken to hospital. I was worried sick that she would pass away. Thankfully she didn't, and I got to see her for the last time.

Unfortunately, K got cancer in her bones and then in her brain. When I got told this from Dad, I felt like crying. Then after that I got told she had only six months to live, which made me feel even worse.

On the first of April 2006, K unfortunately died. That one phone call nearly killed me as I burst into tears. This was more upsetting because it was also my brother's birthday. On the seventh of April, we said our good-byes to the most wonderful and fulfilled person ever. Seeing her eldest son stand up and say a speech was even more depressing. Now I think about her and her family every day and know that she is watching over me.

Adriana writes:

Cancer! Oh what a thing!

Cancer struck my best friend. His name was Raffelle, and he was my nanno. He was the only one who understood me and knew all of my secrets. He died when I was five in 1999 from cancer in the liver. He suffered for three years but said he would never let go.

I remember the last month he was with us was May, and he died the day before my sister's birthday on the twentieth. The last month of his life was always in and out of hospital, and he was always sleeping and depressed. Even though I was only five, I knew it was nearly time to say good-bye. I hated seeing him in this state, but even though he was struggling, he would still get up and play soccer with me.

What made his death more terrible was because he had type II diabetes and his blood pressure would go high and low like the weather in Melbourne (Australia). I remember when his sugar levels were low, he would open a little pack of jelly beans and share them with me. Every afternoon we would go for a walk around the corner and sit on this little white wall, which is still there this very day!

On my way to my nana's, I always stop and sit where he used to sit and think about what life would be like if he was here by my side. On that little wall we have our names from nine years ago, and they are still there.

My nanno was the most loving and generous man in the world. He would do anything for me and my family. Out of all my cousins, I was first in his line. Whenever I think of him, my spirits rise remembering the best man in my life.

Who says kids don't feel someone's illness? These stories were told from the heart, and the whole class listened respectfully when the students read their stories. Fantastic!

I hope you have gained something from these stories since they demonstrate that there are many people who love you and would miss you should you pass away. Imagine how your children, your grandchildren, or any other child relative would feel if *you* passed away. What would they write?

Don't give them a chance to find out. Fight for life. There are many people who will miss your love. Respect yourself, and respect your family. They deserve to have you around for many more years, so take the first step and have a medical checkup.

Finding Out

A Simple Health Check

At age fifty-five, I suppose I was putting on a little weight and could certainly have been fitter, but I felt good about myself and life in general. I had no desire to climb to the top of the ladder as a teacher and felt comfortable in the role of head of school where I led a group of year nine students in a radical education program.

My drinking habits are strictly social, and I don't smoke. In fact, it can be said that I am an extreme anti-smoker and can't understand why people would deliberately indulge in a habit that degrades one's health. Ironic!

I suppose I'm just an average guy. I've never needed to see a doctor and rarely take medicine. Like a lot of men, I believed that if I was not chronically ill, why go to a doctor? I mean, if you've got the flu, all you have to do is wait it out, right? And who needs pills!

This was my attitude. Like I said above, "I'm okay. Nothing's wrong with me. I feel fine. What's the point in seeing a doctor if I don't feel sick!" *I didn't feel any ill effects at all* and thought that going to see a doctor was a waste of time.

My wife, on the other hand, would readily visit our family doctor if she was feeling ill. In fact, she would go for checkups to ensure that she was in a healthy condition. After having four children, she felt comfortable visiting the doctor, and it was nothing for her to have an annual checkup, along with the associated medical tests.

But not me!

We argued regularly about the apparent lack of attention I gave to the state of my health. "Look, when I feel crook, I'll go to the doctor," was my argument, right or wrong. Then one day in the year 2001, my wife said during one of our discussions about my health, "You're fifty-five now. You've never had a cholesterol test. Why not go and at least get that checked out?"

I didn't want to go, but to keep the peace, I agreed, provided she made the appointment.

So here I was one day after school sitting in a doctor's office waiting. I don't like queues at any time, and I don't like, waiting. I knew there was a good reason for not visiting a doctor. I waited forty minutes, probably a normal waiting time but not to an impatient man who couldn't see any reason for the visit in the first place. I was feeling fine, but there I sat, trying to avoid eye contact with the other patients. I read the old magazines and fiddled with my fingers. I gave no thought to the state of my health and never, ever considered cancer in my musings.

"Ian," the doctor called softly. I followed him into the consulting room, mumbling, *"Thank God."*

"How can I help?" he asked once I was seated in a chair on the opposite side of the desk.

"Oh, I'm all right. My wife wants me to have a checkup since I haven't had one in years," I replied confidently.

For the next fifteen minutes or so, the doctor measured my blood pressure, listened to my lungs and heart, and asked questions about the state of my health. One question he asked was about my *urinating* habits and flow rate.

I answered by saying that I occasionally suffered from stage fright, finding it hard to start, and the flow rate varied. Sometimes the urine would trickle out. I sat back confidently and waited for his response. *It's probably old age,* I thought knowingly.

Because of my answer to this question, and since it was my first health test in quite a while, he knew that I had probably never had a check on the state of my prostate so, the next instruction was, "Lower your trousers and underwear, and climb on to the bench." This was said as he put on rubber gloves, so I knew I was in for something special.

I thought, *Shit. The old finger up the bum trick*, so I argued against it.

"Nah, it's all right. There's no need for the test. I'm okay," I reasoned apprehensively, knowing I wouldn't win the argument.

He insisted that I should have the test since he was concerned about my urine flow rate and slow start. Besides, "At your age you are due for the test," he countered against my reasoning.

Bloody hell, I thought as I lowered by trousers before climbing on to the bench to take up the foetal position. I felt very uncomfortable, my heart rate rose significantly, and I felt vulnerable, lying on a small bench with my back to the doctor, waiting for him to stick his finger up my rear end.

"Relax," he said. "You'll only feel a small amount of discomfort."

Relax! How the hell do you relax with someone's finger up your bum?

Nevertheless, I tried to relax by closing my eyes and taking a long, deep breath. I held my breath in anticipation of I don't know what throughout the whole ordeal.

The doctor slid his finger up my anus and began to feel around. Less than a minute later, it was over. All I felt was the movement of his finger pressing on the side of my rectum while he feel tested my prostate. Yes, it was uncomfortable, but there was no pain, just the feeling of a loss of dignity as a result of the test.

"You can get dressed now," he said as he took the gloves off and washed his hands.

I dressed quickly and sat waiting in anticipation for the result of the test.

"Your prostate is swollen. It may mean nothing. The prostate can enlarge a little with age, but it can mean other things. My concern at this time is to eliminate the chance that it may be cancer of the prostate," the doctor explained matter-of-factly.

The C-word. Cancer. *Shit!* I thought as my heart beat rapidly because of increased anxiety. My head seemed to be swimming in a sea of negativity as I thought about this word. *Cancer—don't people die from this?*

He picked up a form used to specify blood tests and started to write. "I want you to have a blood test as soon as possible. I want you to have a test for PSA levels, cholesterol, and sugar. You can't eat anything before the test, so it would be best to go early in the morning."

"What's PSA?" I asked as I recovered from the digital rectal examination (DRE) experience.

"Prostate-specific antigen. It's a protein produced by the prostate," he replied. "If blood levels are too high, it's a fair indication that there may be cancer. The test isn't accurate, but it's the best there is at the moment."

He assured me that he was only erring on the side of caution and that indeed there might not be anything untoward about my enlarged prostate. But this didn't make me feel any better. He had linked the PSA levels with cancer, something I had never thought about. Hell, I just wanted a simple health test.

As I drove home, I reflected on the fact that I *might* have a cancer. It certainly didn't make me feel too good about the prospect since I knew nothing at all about cancer of the prostate. I only knew that cancer can lead to death, and this limited knowledge didn't make me feel confident. Bloody hell! I didn't know anyone with cancer.

I felt morbid. I imagined myself with cancer of the prostate, whatever that might mean, and came up with a picture of myself lying in bed with my family crying around me. I didn't listen to the radio on the way home, which was my usual custom. I wanted peace and quiet, time to *wallow in self-pity,* and I hadn't even had the blood test yet!

I swore and thumped the steering wheel. *Shit! Cancer. Why me?* I thought. My life was over! I would never be the same.

Ah, ignorance! What a poor excuse for a man of reasoning I portrayed at that moment.

My wife was, of course, sympathetic and urged that I have the blood tests as soon as possible. Since there was a diagnostic clinic close to work, I went early next morning before going to school.

Now! I had never ever had a blood test before, so the wait in the clinic was also an ordeal. The nurse called my name, and I followed her into a room. In my mind's eye, all I could see was a needle going into my arm, and I hate needles. "Just a little prick," the nurse said, inserting a needle into a vein she found in the crease of my elbow.

As she inserted the needle, my toes wriggled madly in anticipation of the pain. I also held my breath as I watched, but all I felt was a slight pressure, so I relaxed.

I watched as blood surged into the vial, and then she removed it and filled another one. The nurse was right. It was just a little prick, and before long, the ordeal was over. Little to no pain—that's how I like it.

I drove to school and spoke to nobody about my plight, but the staff knew that something was on my mind, and with a little coaxing, they gained the information that had occupied my mind. "So you've only just had the blood test?" a staff member asked.

"Yes," I replied.

"So what are you worried about? You said the doctor told you that it is a precaution and the likelihood for the swelling may be something else," I was told matter of factly. Everyone else agreed, so I decided to relax a little and not worry, at least until the results were in.

Two days later, the results were in. I called the doctor and arranged to see him, hoping for some good news.

I sat in the waiting room in anticipation of what he would tell me. I didn't care about the sugar and cholesterol levels; all I wanted to know was if I had cancer. I didn't rehearse any scenarios in my mind, just in case. I just sat there, my heart thumping while I fidgeted in my seat.

"Ian," I heard the doctor say softly and with a smile.

I took a deep breath and followed him nervously into his consulting room.

He read the report while I waited anxiously, all the while trying to look calm. "The blood tests indicate that your sugar is normal and your cholesterol is elevated slightly," he said.

Yeah, yeah, get on with it. What about the PSA? I heard myself saying in my head.

Then he said, "Your PSA level is elevated, so I want you to go and see a specialist (an urologist) who specialises in such conditions."

The doctor wrote a referral and handed it to me, again reassuring me that it didn't necessarily mean cancer but could be something else.

Something else? Hell, what does that mean? To a healthy specimen such as myself, I didn't want something else or cancer!

"It's highly likely that the elevated PSA levels are due to the disease benign prostactic hyperplasia (BPH), which is very common for your age group," the doctor assured me as we walked from his office.

But along with the doctor's reassurance, I still wasn't convinced! *Why see a specialist? Don't these guys only come out to play when something's wrong?* I thought. Such was the quality of my normally, rational thinking. I was doomed, and my GP didn't want to tell me. He was leaving it up to the specialist.

The drive home from the doctor's office was, once more, full of doom and gloom, but by the time I had arrived home, I had managed to put on a brave face. No need to alarm my wife; however, you wouldn't have thought this if you had been in the car with me.

But wives have a way of knowing how husbands feel, and she was very supportive. "The doctor told you that it could be *something else,* so don't worry," she said sympathetically. "Let's wait and see. You're probably worrying for nothing."

This is what my teaching colleagues had said! Hey, *maybe I was overreacting.*

I took my wife's advice and tried not to worry about it until I had seen the specialist. The time passed quicker than I could imagine without any further thoughts of having cancer. I focused on the job and my students.

Addendum: Normal levels of PSA vary with age, the upper limit being lower for men younger than fifty (less than 4ng/ml). If, at age fifty-five (or thereabout) the level of PSA is below 4ng/ml, the possibility for contracting cancer of the prostate is about 15 percent. If levels are between 4 and 10ng/ml, the rate increases to 25 percent, and if the levels of PSA are higher than 10 ng/ml, the chances of contracting the disease increases to 60+ percent.

Please remember, a PSA test is not a conclusive test for determining whether you, or your partner, have cancer of the prostate. PSA levels can rise because of a urinary infection or the disease benign prostatic hyperplasia (BPH).

Meeting the Urologist

One week later, I was sitting in another waiting room, waiting (and waiting) to see the urologist. While waiting, I secretly studied the other patients. Were they going to see the specialist for the same reason as me? The waiting room had a certain amount of morbidity about it, probably because if you are seeing a specialist, then there may be something wrong. My mood matched the thinking I experienced in the waiting room.

God! Everyone's as old as, or older than, me, I thought as I surveyed the other patients, occasionally smiling if one caught my eye.

At long last, I was called into the consulting room. I waited ninety minutes, and I wasn't happy. I suppose there is nothing that could be done, particularly when you are consulting a doctor about a problem that can be associated with the prostate.

After a short amount of small talk by way of introduction, the specialist got to the point. "Your PSA level is elevated and is a concern for me." He got out of his chair and proceeded to put on rubber gloves.

You guessed it, another DRE or finger-up-the-bum test. Once again, my heart rate sped up in anticipation. Once again, I was anxious for no reason since the inspection was over in a very quick time and with only a small amount of discomfort. But it's all about the dignity thing and the feeling of being invaded.

"Your prostate is enlarged," he said as he removed the gloves. "It's still not clear whether there is a cancer present or whether you are suffering from prostatitis or benign prostatic hyperplasia (BPH)."

These terms meant nothing to me except that they were not cancerous, but offered the same symptoms as prostate cancer. My hope was renewed though, since, for my age group (over fifty), BPH was a strong possibility.

I listened in anticipation as the doctor got a pencil from the drawer and began to draw a schematic diagram of the prostate to show me how prostatitis and BPH acted on the prostate. One thing was certain; doctors need to have art lessons. I watched and listened with a voice in my head saying, *You have cancer. Forget the other stuff.*

An inflamed prostate can squeeze the urethra, restricting urine flow. Both prostatitis and BPH can be treated using an antibiotic, but in BPH, it may be necessary to have a small operation where a section of the prostate is removed around the urethra to relieve the pressure, thus enlarging the urethra and allowing urine to flow freely while removing the discomfort. This operation is called a trans-urethral resection of the prostate (or TURPs), a fancy term to indicate that a small section of the prostate is removed to enlarge the urethra. The procedure usually requires a short stay in hospital, and a catheter is installed through the penis for a short time. More on this later.

The urethra is a tube that carries urine from the bladder and exits through the penis. It passes through the prostate.

Young men (younger than fifty) are not likely to encounter BPH but can suffer from prostatitis. A course of antibiotics usually cures prostatitis. Both diseases cause an increase in the size of the prostate.

At least now I had something other than cancer to hang my hopes upon. BPH still sounded like an unpleasant prospect, but it was not life threatening. To me, it was the lesser of two evils, so I took on board the fact that I might have BPH and relaxed while the specialist described all prospects, including what my inner voice was telling me, cancer.

At the end of the discussion, the doctor said, "To limit the possibilities, I would like to perform a biopsy, which will require day surgery."

Hey! Why not? Anything to eliminate cancer from the prognosis. I had been in hospital before; after all, I had my tonsils out when I was a small child.

I readily agreed to the biopsy and left the consulting room with a certain amount of trepidation but optimistic about the prospects. I tried to block out the option of cancer of the prostate, taking on the belief that men of my age and older are very likely to develop BPH.

Ah! Life was beginning to look rosy once more. The tests so far had not definitely indicated cancer.

I drove home confident that I only had BPH. I even sang along with what was playing on the radio. It would appear that time had improved my outlook.

Biopsy

One week later, I was admitted into hospital for day surgery. While waiting for the doctor, a nurse approached and said that she was going to administer an enema, which I vehemently protested.

"I've used my bowels," I said, but to no avail.

She pulled out a syringe that contained a liquid substance and directed me to lie on the bench while she inserted the syringe up my anus and injected the enema. Another moment of indignity! Come on, now, I know I have a cute butt, but!

I sat on a chair in a surgical gown, waiting for the enema to work.

As I anticipated, it did nothing, but I suppose the nursing staff can't take risks. "Hospital rules," she said.

"Yeah, yeah," I replied.

Twenty minutes later, I was lying in the foetal position—yes, you guessed it, first with a DRE followed closely by a camera. *Yes, a camera!* Once more I felt nervous, more so since I was having a biopsy. My heart raced, and I talked nervously with the doctor.

The biopsy involved inserting a small camera up through the anus so that the doctor could survey the area. Small ultrasound signals were emitted from the device, which were interpreted by the camera, or detection device, as an image of my prostate and surrounding tissues.

The doctor manoeuvred the device to gain an overall picture of the prostate, which incidentally was shown on a monitor. I was awake to see the images and to discuss what would happen during the biopsy. General anaesthetic is also available if you don't want to know what's going on, but I wanted to know what was happening.

I'm certainly glad that the doctor knew what he was looking at. All I could see was tissue of various shades of grey. I saw the needle being fired as it darted across the field of view.

In truth, the whole affair was quite painless. The device was about two centimetres in diameter, and it had a central chamber where long needles could be placed to secure small samples when fired into the prostate.

I watched and listened with interest. The doctor showed me the needle he intended to fire at the prostate. *Why so large?* I thought as I surveyed the intimidating object, but it needed to be long so that it could be retrieved easily after firing.

The needle was spring loaded, and when fired at the prostate, it would strike the target area and then pull back into the device, where it was removed to retrieve the sample. Seven such needles were shot into various locations of my prostate, each retrieving samples, which I had hoped would be cancer free.

Oh, by the way, all I could feel of the needles taking the sample was slight pressure. No pain! Fantastic.

After the procedure, I got dressed and went home. Since I didn't have a general anaesthetic, I didn't need to stay in hospital for observation.

Up to This Stage, What Had I Learnt?

First, it is important for me to have regular checks on the state of my health, since "feeling great" may not reflect the true state of my health.

Second, the DRE was not as demoralising as I first thought. If I had been too proud or too much of a man to endure the indignity of having someone's finger poked up my bum, then you wouldn't be reading this article now. I'd probably not be on this planet!

Third, the subsequent tests were essential to determine whether cancer was the cause of the swelling of the prostate. The swelling may not have been caused by cancer cells, *which for many men is the likely situation.* Under such circumstances, a corrective procedure can be performed to reduce the inflammation and to increase the urine flow.

Fourth, the biopsy was not the ordeal I thought it would be. It was pain free and nowhere near as imposing as first thought.

Fifth, having learnt that I indeed had cancer of the prostate (disclosed below), I discovered that it was not the end of the world and that life goes on, even for me.

Let's continue the journey.

The Biopsy Report

About ten days after the biopsy, I returned to see the specialist. The news wasn't good, but he made me feel that the end of the world was not at hand.

I tried to act cool when he told me the results of the biopsy, trying to make it sound like it was just another disease, but inside, my guts were in turmoil.

Shit! Bloody cancer. What does this mean? Hell. I could die! I thought as my heart raced while my face maintained an expression of highly stressed nonchalance, strained though it was. I even managed a smile.

"The needlepoint samples returned four with cancer, one of which was on the margin," the specialist explained. I listened in a state of minor turmoil.

"Mmm," I said, trying to sound as if I understood what he was saying while all the time, I was thinking of the possible consequences, including death. I leant over his desk and watched in panicked casualness as he drew diagrams showing the suspected sites.

The thoughts I experienced are natural, as was my outward behaviour to remain cool under the circumstances. In fact, if I had broken down, this too would have been normal behaviour. We are all different in temperament, and each individual has a variety of views about the situation at hand; therefore, we all react differently. The hardest thing for me was to tell my wife!

Strangely, I remember little about that particular doctor's appointment, other than the fact that I was told I had cancer and other small snippets alluded to above, but the subsequent appointments remain clear in my memory.

The drive home was uneventful as far as driving was concerned, but my mood was sour. I swore and carried on as if I was about to die tomorrow, and the steering wheel took a lot of thumping. As I got closer to home, I tried to calm myself down. I tried to regain the persona I reflected in the doctor's office, but I was too worked up. My head was swimming with visions of cancer. I was doomed.

When at last I arrived home, my wife said empathetically, "So, what happened?"

That was it! I was a blubbering wreck for a few minutes while I tried to tell her that the diagnosis was positive for cancer. But never since! After a few moments, I regained my composure and told her what the doctor had told me. I took deep breaths as I repeated what the doctor had disclosed. She was quiet but accepted my explanation. What else could she do? She was the rock who supported me while I wallowed in self-pity.

We discussed the situation well into the night, with me adding an occasional negative comment, but in the end, we decided not to get too carried away with our emotions until we had spoken with the specialist the following week.

The ensuring time was spent with good wishes from relatives and friends, all saying, "Well, you must look after yourself," and "If I can help, give me a call," whatever that might mean. But I suppose I would have said something similar.

How often do you hear words like, "If you need something, just give me a call"? What would the person who uttered the words do if I asked for help, and what help could he or she give? What do you say to such comments? "Thanks, I will," or "Thank you."

The truth is, friends and relatives mean well and are a tremendous support during this time of stress. They can, indeed, help you to see that life goes on. You don't need to suffer. I didn't see any point in hiding my condition from anyone. Silence would have meant going through my own personal hell alone and with irrationally created images. Friends help you to see reason.

If you are diagnosed with cancer of the prostate, or any other debilitating disease, for that matter, *tell others*. Apart from the usual support statements, you will be pleasantly surprised at the actual level of support you'll receive.

I didn't tell the staff at school about the outcome of my visit with the specialist. I didn't have to. I was quiet, and I suppose I behaved differently and the staff figured out the outcome for themselves. Nevertheless, they were extremely supportive and in fact took over doing a lot of my normal jobs. See! People will understand and support you.

Options Given

At last, the appointed time to meet with the urologist arrived. My wife and I met with the doctor, who was, as usual, very positive in his manner generally and with regard to any questions I asked.

He drew diagrams indicating the sites where the active cancer was found. Out of the seven needles fired at the prostate, four came back positive, one of the cancers being located on the margin of the prostate, which he said, "Might present problems."

I, of course, focused on these words and started to create an image of myself with problems.

"The diagnosis is not a death sentence. Cancer of the prostate is generally located entirely within the prostate and as such, usually affords excellent survival opportunities," the specialist explained.

It is important to realise that no doctor can give a 100 percent guarantee of survival once the prostate, along with the cancer, is removed. He quoted figures of 80 to 90 percent, which were good odds. A range of figures will probably be given to you should a biopsy turn out to be positive, but please, do not rationalise that the odds will work against you. After the discussion, I preferred to think that I would be one of the 80 to 90 percent who survived. Trust your doctor, not your thoughts or misguided perceptions.

Having explained that the diagnosis was not a death sentence, the specialist then explained the nature of the cancer. I was considered to be relatively young at the age of fifty-five, and the younger a person is when diagnosed with this disease, the faster the cancer grows. "If you had been diagnosed at the age of seventy-five, we probably wouldn't do anything, since the growth rate is very slow at this age. You would probably die of old age, not the cancer," he explained.

But I'm not seventy-five! I thought, *And I have a cancer on the margin.*

"However, in younger men, the cancer is more aggressive and will grow more rapidly, with the possibility of metastasising (breaking up) and spreading to other sites. It is important to get the cancer now, while it is located entirely within the prostate."

Now I know where you're heading. You're going to be very sick, I continued, but my thinking was wrong. I was so full of self-pity and "Why did this happen to me?" that I didn't quite understand what I was being told. It wasn't until the operation was over and I had time to reflect that I understood what the doctor was telling me.

If you are younger than fifty and have a suspicion about the health of your prostate as determined by decreased urine flow, frequent night visits to the toilet, difficulty starting or stopping the urine flow, associated pain, or decreased libido (sex drive), then I suggest you take the appropriate tests—*now.*

Back to my situation.

Once the specialist was sure that my wife and I had understood the situation to this point, as indicated by the occasional nod or "aha," he explained the options, one of which I had to choose. He also recommended that the decision be made in partnership with my wife, not alone. After all, she had to endure the consequences as much as me.

Four options were proposed, and the doctor described each in detail. For the purposes of this book, I have provided a *brief* overview of each option to satisfy your curiosity. Your doctor will be able to give a more detailed description to satisfy any queries you have concerning the options, particularly when you have decided on which option to take. I advise you to *write down* any questions concerning your situation and the options before consulting with the specialist so you know precisely what to expect.

Watchful waiting: This consisted of doing nothing while being constantly monitored through blood samples and the DRE. This option is most often used for men who are older than seventy-five, since the rate of growth of the cancer is much slower. If it becomes a problem, then one of the other options can be considered. My uncle was diagnosed with cancer of the prostate at age eighty-five; he has since died, but not from cancer.

Brachytherapy: This procedure involves the use of radioactive "seeds" that are injected into the prostate (about one hundred seeds), thus radiating the prostate and destroying the cancer cells. Like any procedure, it is important to realise that the process cannot guarantee 100 percent success, so you should be guided by your doctor. The radiation is localised, so the tissue around the prostate remains healthy. Brachytherapy is used in cancers that are located within one region of the prostate, which is often the case for cancer of the prostate. A possible side effect is impotence, though it is at a lower rate than that for a radical prostatectomy. Brachytherapy involves a day stay in hospital, and the patient can return to work soon after, based on the doctor's advice.

Radiotherapy: This is also known as external beam radiation and involves radiating a localised area with x-rays. More often than not, the radiation is initiated from more than one direction so the surrounding tissue is not damaged and the target site receives the bulk of the radiation.

Like brachytherapy, this treatment is given for cancer that is located entirely within the prostate. It is also offered as a preferred treatment after a radical prostatectomy if the cancer was not eliminated during the surgery. Possible side effects of this treatment include a burning sensation when urinating, diarrhoea, and bleeding of the bowel, all of which return to normal soon after the treatment. It may also be offered along with hormone treatment. Radiotherapy is usually given over a number of weeks to help maintain the health of the patient. If you need this treatment, you will be required to attend a radiotherapy clinic daily. More on this treatment later.

Radical Prostatectomy: This is the surgical removal of the prostate. The idea behind this procedure is, if the prostate is removed, then it can be reasonably assumed that the cancer is also removed. Unfortunately, if the cancer is located on the margin of the prostate, then some cells may remain after removal of the prostate and will require further treatment, usually radiotherapy. This procedure involves a stay in the hospital of about six days, depending on the circumstances and your doctor. The operation involves making an incision in the region from just below the bellybutton to the pelvic area. An alternative procedure involves keyhole surgery where the prostate is removed through a smaller incision. If you have keyhole surgery, you can expect your stay in hospital to be shorter, and there will be minimum damage to your body since the incisions are small.

The above procedures were offered to me by my specialist. Other treatments (not offered to me) may be presented to you, depending on the staging of the cancer:

Chemotherapy: Treatment with drugs that destroy the cancer cells. Regional chemotherapy involves administering the drugs to the site, here, the prostate gland. If the cancer has spread beyond the prostate, then systemic chemotherapy is given where the drug is injected into the bloodstream to be disseminated to all parts of the body.

It is important to note that the drug used in chemotherapy can also destroy normal body tissue. Fortunately, because *cancer cells grow more rapidly than normal cells*, they *absorb* the drug more readily and are consequently destroyed more quickly than normal cells, thus minimising the damage to normal cells.

Radiotherapy and hormone treatment: Radiotherapy was briefly described above. It is often used alone but can be used in conjunction with hormone therapy, particularly if the cancer is located on the margin of the prostate or if there is a possibility that it may have spread.

Prostate cancer cells are often affected by the male hormone *testosterone*, which is produced in the testes. Testosterone can cause the cancer cells to grow, so if the testosterone levels are reduced to zero, there is a strong possibility that the growth of the cancer cells will be arrested and the cancer itself may shrink. One certain way to eliminate the production of testosterone is to undergo surgical castration, a real option, but do you want this? Hormone treatment mimics surgical castration without the loss of the testicles.

Hormone treatment can consist of one or both of the following. An anti-androgen tablet taken orally (Androcur) *blocks the action* of testosterone without preventing its production. Taken with Zoladex, a luteinizing hormone-releasing hormone (LHRH) analog or agonists, which is injected just under the skin or into the muscle and which *prevents the production* of testosterone, they provide an effective mechanism to minimise cancer growth.

It Won't Happen to Me

Having been diagnosed with prostate cancer, I became concerned for my brothers and sons. I told my brothers about my situation and suggested that they go see their doctor and have the appropriate tests. "Yeah for sure," one said. "No one's going to stick a finger up my a ..." the other replied.

I had the prostatectomy operation in November 2001. My youngest brother decided to have the tests in 2005. At this time, my other brother still refused to have the test, but his resolve was weakening.

Why wait? If a family member has been diagnosed with cancer, then the odds are in favour of siblings also having or contracting the cancer. *Fear* is one reason why a person may not take the warning seriously, and I believe the perception of having someone invade your body with an apparent loss of dignity may also be a strong reason.

So why is it important to have the test, you might ask?

When my youngest brother had the digital rectal examination (DRE), he was told that his prostate seemed to be of normal size. He told the doctor about my situation, so a PSA test was ordered, which registered normal levels of PSA.

Up to this point, any male would be happy with the results, but because of my predicament, the doctor arranged for my brother to have an ultrasound and a biopsy. The ultrasound came back negative, but the biopsy recorded four counts of cancer out of six needle samples. A significant result indeed!

He has since undergone a radical prostatectomy. What if he had stopped after the first two tests? It was quite justifiable! By the way, my brother's PSA count remains at zero, a significant result for a person who has had a prostatectomy. His attitude is similar to mine; that is, he expects to live his life into old age.

My other brother, now having two brothers with prostate cancer, has reconsidered his decision and will have the tests, but when? Is it out of fear or bravado that he hasn't been tested?

What about yourself?

You cannot be certain that you are free from cancer unless you have the appropriate tests. If the tests are negative, then watchful waiting is the way to go. *Get tested every year or two.*

Consider the Following Scenario

You are a healthy forty-year-old with a wife and two kids. You work out at the gym, play soccer, and ride a bike to work each day. In other words, you are a picture of health with a model family. You love your wife and kids and look forward to seeing them every night; they are your life's blood. It could be said that you and your wife are key players in your social set. People love to be around you, and your strength and character can be relied upon.

Life is wonderful until one day, you have a test for cancer of the prostate that, unfortunately, comes back positive. Your doctor suggests that you have a life-saving operation. You reflect back on your life and see a strong, masculine image of yourself. Your sex life is great, and the people around you know what a great sports person you are. You consider these facts in making the decision.

Five years later, your wife is crying at your grave site.

Do you know the odd thing about this story? It is true! A friend had a strong, masculine image of himself, and life without good sex was not an option for him. So he took a punt but unfortunately lost. Is it realistic to leave a family without a father and supporter just because you want to protect your image? Is your masculinity and being seen to be masculine so vital to you that you will protect it until death? You know what? This is one question you have to answer should you be required to proceed with treatment for cancer of the prostate.

PS: My other brother has had a prostate checkup and has been given the all clear. Good news indeed.

My Choice

The doctor's explanation of the various options was both graphic and detailed. As I said earlier, he explained to my wife and me that part of the cancer was on the margin and that this might present a problem. However, the choice to make was mine and my wife's. He offered no recommendation until I asked for it.

Needless to say, both my wife and I were anxious about the situation, and based on the evidence and options presented to us, we decided to go with the radical prostatectomy, which he suggested would be the surest method for eliminating the cancer based on current thinking. The logic my wife and I used in rationalising the decision was that if the cancer was entirely within the prostate, then the removal of the prostate should eliminate the cancerous cells. But we were concerned about the cancer reported to be on the margin. We hoped that it too would be removed.

The specialist emphasised the fact that with prostate removal, the nerve responsible for causing erections would more than likely be severed or damaged and consequently, normal sex might not be available. One thing was certain—the climax would be different since semen cannot be produced, but a climax is assuredly reached if you are capable of having sex. I was told that I might need to use a vacuum pump (yes, you read it correctly) or ingest Viagra to gain anything that might resemble an erection.

Having chosen to have a radical prostatectomy is not to say that the other procedures would not have been just as effective. It was my choice to make, and my thinking (along with that of my wife) led to the decision my wife and I chose.

Even though the doctor gave us a week to think about the options and to come up with an option, we made the decision during the meeting. I just wanted to get it over with.

We discussed the procedure a little further before the doctor set a date for the operation. The date was set for three weeks from the meeting (November 2001) so I could give blood for the operation. When your own blood is used during the operation, this is called autonomous blood and therefore limits complications associated with blood transfusions during the operation. It is not a necessary requirement, so be guided by your doctor should you reach this point.

A three-week wait time was set for the operation since I needed to give blood once a week for three weeks, thus giving three units of blood.

The next three weeks dragged by slowly, and as luck had it, I developed a cold two weeks before the operation, which threatened postponement. In the end, because of the cold, I only gave two units of blood, which was considered adequate.

So what about the cold?

I coughed and sniffled my way through the week, willing it to go away. "Bloody hell! They'll postpone the operation. This could put me back weeks," I said to my wife, looking for answers to my dilemma.

One week before the operation, I visited the specialist and because I seemed to be feeling better, and I had *said* that I was feeling better, the operation proceeded as planned. *Thank God*, I thought. A wave of relief washed over me, and I set about preparing myself, psychologically, for the operation. Unfortunately, I had also developed a persistent cough, which I didn't tell the doctor about. It produced complications. Read on.

Prostate Removal

The Operation

With bag packed and breakfast forgone, I finally arrived at the hospital at about eleven thirty in the morning. The operation was planned for late afternoon.

Having had no breakfast and no planned meals for quite a while, it was with a rumbling stomach that I met with the case manager, a trained nurse who was obviously well versed in post-operative procedures. Meeting this lady was helpful since she managed to help me relax and feel good about the procedure I was about to undergo.

My wife stayed with me during this time. In fact, she stayed until I went under the anaesthetic, and this too was comforting. Involve your wife or partner. It's important that he or she feels comfortable with the procedure and can see that you are coping. Waiting at home for a phone call would be traumatic. Share the experience.

Time seemed to drag by. I checked my watch often, though I don't know why since I didn't even know when the operation was going to take place. I was given an enema, and once more, it did nothing. My wife and I sat in the ward, waiting. I began to get more anxious and became fidgety, but with my wife present, I managed to produce some semblance of calm.

Having an operation was a new experience for me. This was the first time since I was five years old that I was a patient in a hospital, and I experienced mixed emotions. I was happy because I was having the cancer removed and nervous because of the operation and the pain I thought I'd experience later.

All I was allowed to drink was small quantities of water; it had something to do with having anaesthetic. For a short time, I sat and waited by myself while my wife went to get something to eat. During this time, I managed to live various scenarios in my mind, some negative and some good. "What if," was on the agenda at that moment, and these played in my mind constantly.

I tried to read a book, but to no avail. When my wife finally returned from her lunch break, she could see that I'd been in thought about the operation and weaved her magic to calm me once more.

At midafternoon, I was given a surgical gown, which signified to me that the time for the operation was imminent. Instant anxiety. I joked about the backward gown, but inside, my empty stomach churned and my heart raced.

Time seemed to fly by, and I have very little recollection of when the events occurred. I supposed that because of the anxiety, clock watching might have worked to increase it even more, along with the amount of forgetfulness. I watched the clock earlier but stopped when I realised what I was doing to myself.

During the long period of waiting, the anaesthetist visited me. I was weighed, and he told me about his role during the operation and the fact that he would be present for the entire time. He also gave me two options for managing pain after the operation. There was self-management, where I would be given a device that, when I felt pain, I would press a button and release morphine to manage the pain. The second method was to have an epidural, where an opiate would be administered automatically, and consequently, I would be pain free all the time. I took this option.

Inserting the epidural was a delicate procedure. I was first given a local anaesthetic in my back before the fun began. Since a catheter had to be inserted into the epidural space, which was very close to the spine and which is a very thin region, I wasn't allowed to move. An assistant held

31

my arms while I sat on the edge of the bed while he pulled me forward, holding me still until the catheter had been inserted.

The procedure involved first carefully inserting a needle in my back and ultimately into the epidural space, and then the catheter was inserted up the needle and the needle removed. The catheter was taped to my back so it couldn't be accidentally removed or slip out.

I remember sitting on the bed and being pulled forward, but I didn't feel a thing. Great!

That done, I lay back on the bed and waited. An hour or so later, the anaesthetist came and gave me a mild sedative, or so he said, since when I woke up, the operation was over. I knew and felt nothing. What a tricky anaesthetist!

During the operation and before the prostate was removed, the lymph node near the groin was removed and analysed. If it showed evidence of prostate cancer cells, the operation would not have proceeded any further, since this would have been significant evidence that the cancer had spread. Luckily for me, there was no such evidence, so the operation proceeded. My prostate was removed.

After the operation when I woke in the intensive care unit, I looked around and listened to the sounds around me. Soft music was playing, and an intensive care nurse was taking my blood pressure. Every hour or earlier the nurse went through his procedure, ensuring my safety. He asked me questions, but I don't recall what they were. I was oblivious to what was happening around me. As far as I was concerned, I was the only person in the room, possibly even the universe. I felt nothing, just peaceful oblivion.

As I regained my faculties, we began to talk more, and I noticed that there were other people in the room. In fact, the room was a hive of activity. All of a sudden, there was noise. I could hear the hum of equipment and the sounds of nurses talking to the patients in their care. What happened to the quiet?

I was still not allowed to eat or drink. I sucked ice cubes to relieve the thirst, which I must say was quite intense.

Since I didn't feel any pain, I didn't ask about the operation, nor did I bother to look. I was blissfully unaware of what had happened. I just lay in bed without any concern, listening to the sounds around me.

Sometime during my stay in intensive care, my wife, my sister-in-law, and one of my daughters came to visit. They stayed only long enough to see that I was okay. I was drifting in and out of consciousness, so there was no point in them hanging around, and I daresay they wouldn't have gotten a decent conversation from me.

Once I was fully awake and the nurse was certain that I was in no danger, I was removed from intensive care and taken to a ward. I wanted a private room, but shared rooms were an option.

In my new, wakened state, I took the opportunity to study my body. There were four tubes exiting from various parts of my body: one for the epidural, another for saline solution and antibiotics, another a drip feed, and of course, the catheter, which was put into position up through my penis to the bladder during the operation. A drain tube also hung off the side of my stomach with a drain bag collecting fluid. Each tube was necessary, and I didn't feel any discomfort.

I also became aware of the fact that I was naked. I dressed as quickly as I could given the circumstances, but I needed assistance, so modesty was thrown out the door. Hey, there was no chance that I would embarrass myself by producing an erection. A penis with a drip bag is not a desirable image.

However, getting into bed was a chore while I tried not to pull any of the tubes and ensure that they didn't get tangled. Now that I wore pyjamas, they added to the dilemma. For the rest of that day, I simply lay in bed and rested. Nurses measured my vital signs regularly and ensured my comfort. But still, no meals or drinks.

I even had a shower during this day. I was assisted by a nurse to a plastic chair where I sat while taking a shower. The wound was covered with a sanitised, plastic material to keep the water away from the operation site. The nurse returned to help me dress since, given the number of tubes, assistance was certainly required and I was feeling tired. The effects of the epidural made me a little uncertain on my feet.

An operation certainly takes a lot out of you. Since I couldn't feel pain, it was easy for me to believe that I should be able to walk around. But that wasn't to be! I was exhausted and needed rest. So I lay in bed, watching a myriad of spiders walk across the top of the doorway. They walked in unison and rhythmically, and on more than one occasion, I had to ask a nurse or a visitor if they could see them. Of course they didn't exist, but they looked so real. During one of my wife's visits, I asked her if the walls of the room had a herringbone pattern. They didn't and were painted in a pale yellow/brown. I was assured by the nurses that I hadn't gone mad and what I saw was just the result of the epidural. I was hallucinating, or if you like, I was on a controlled trip. It's strange how you view the world when your faculties are not in normal working order.

During the second day, I went for a walk around the hospital wing. I had to take the machinery for administering the epidural, along with the drip feed, antibiotics, and drainage bags, with me. The catheter bag was strapped to my leg, so it wasn't a pretty sight. I wasn't the only one in this position however, so I didn't feel too much out of place, just a little self-conscious.

I remember visiting my mother in hospital about forty years previously, and the scenario was very different. The wards were darker, and mum lay in bed until she was discharged. Ah, the changes in health care. Aren't they marvellous?

The initial walk was short and very tiring, but I walked twice more during that day, increasing the length each time. My strength was returning slowly, but I still hadn't had anything to eat. Strangely enough, I didn't feel hungry; the drip feed did its job.

For most of the day, I either read a book or watched TV. Thankfully, I didn't get bored. I was visited by the specialist who was happy with the outcome of the operation, and nurses constantly monitored my vital signs. I suppose there wasn't time to get bored.

Since I had a single room, I didn't have anyone else to talk to, but it is my nature to be alone. It gave me time to recall all that had happened and to plan my future. Yes, I actually thought about going back to work and what that might entail.

On the third day, the epidural was removed. It had managed the pain effectively. I felt no pain! In fact, with the epidural, I couldn't feel anything from my navel to my knees since this was the region targeted to minimise the pain. During the day, a nurse would come into the room with a block of ice and place it on various parts of my body within the specified region, asking if I could feel the coldness of the ice. Not a thing. Zip.

Once the epidural was removed, normal sensations slowly returned, and for the first time, I could feel the pain that had been so effectively masked. It wasn't too severe. At first, for the remainder of that day and night, I was given morphine injections that stopped the pain. The following day however, this option was removed, and pain control continued by first taking panadene forte, then panadene, and finally, panadol.

I was surprised at how effectively these common pain control tablets managed the pain. Yes, there may have been dull aches, but most of the time, I was pain free except maybe when I over-stretched or coughed.

Ah yes, remember my cold? I didn't want the operation to be cancelled, so I lied a little about my cold. The symptoms seemed to have disappeared, but the cough remained and this caused problems.

In fact, I had to be taught how to cough since it was persistent. Yes, I actually had to be taught to cough. No hard, retching stuff, no. I had to hold my stomach tightly and "huff" the cough out. Occasionally, a deep, hardy cough couldn't be controlled, so the ultimate price of having the operation when I wasn't fully fit was that my *wound opened*. A small, circular opening, about the size of a fifty-cent piece developed because of my insistence to have the operation. It was nobody's fault but my own.

God! I'll have to be sown up again, I thought. No!

The wound was cleaned daily, and with the passing of time, the gaping hole filled and healed itself. This process took *two months*. Nurses had to come to my home to continue monitoring its healing process, including Christmas day! I wouldn't look at the wound since it appeared to me when I first saw it that it would tear all the way up the cut. All I could see was raw meat, and this meat was me. It was a lesson well learnt, but too late. It wasn't until one week before I had to return to work in January that the nurses stopped their home visits. Ah, such is life.

Back to my situation.

After seven days in hospital, I was released on the provision that the hospital home visit, nursing service attend my needs. No problem! I knew they were needed. After all, I had a hole in my stomach that needed filling.

After signing the release papers, I walked slowly to the car, carrying my urine drainage bag. Yes, the catheter remained until about three weeks after the operation. To put it into perspective, I had the drainage bag strapped to my leg so it was hidden. At night, I would use a larger bag that hung off the side of my bed. No more trips to the toilet.

In case you're wondering why a catheter is necessary when the prostate is removed, the urethra has to be stitched up to connect to the bladder. Time is required to allow it to heal, and if urine is allowed to flow through the urethra, it is possible that an infection will occur. The catheter prevents this from happening since the urine flows through the plastic tubing.

For a short time after my release from hospital, I continued to cough, but happily, it was subsiding. I slept uneasily the first night. It was difficult to find a comfortable position with the drainage bag hanging over the side of the bed. I feared rolling over, asleep, and tangling the drainage line, so I lie in bed on my back or facing the outside with my leg hanging over the side.

The home nurse service came to my home early each morning to dress the wound. Over the three-month period, I had four different nurses visit me, but as was the situation in hospital, the nurses were great. During each visit, they would explain what they were doing and were gentle with their actions. The visiting nurse also had to monitor the warfarin levels, since I had to have my blood thinned. Why? Ha! The cough wreaked more damage than I thought. Read on.

During the second night home, disaster struck.

I tried sleeping sitting up since my chest hurt. There's a sign for you. I sat in bed with the drainage tube over the side with pillows packed around me. I was comfortable but breathed uneasily, and sleep was impossible because of the pain in my chest, so when the nurse came to dress my wound, I told her about the pain and this rang alarm bells for her. She suspected a *blood clot* and directed me back to hospital, where I had a CAT scan.

A blood clot was found on my lung. One tiny clot caused so much pain. Lying on the table during the CAT scan caused immense discomfort and pain. "Don't move," the technician said as I lay with my chest bearing down on me while I tried not to move or cough. But hey, I'd had the operation. God knew when I'd get better, though.

I lay on the table with the mechanism close to my chest, trying to hold my breath while the technician processed an image. I felt more pain and discomfort as a result of the blood clot than I did from the operation! Ah, the irony of it all.

The CAT scan was taken at about mid-morning and as a consequence of what the image displayed, the decision was made to re-admit me into hospital. Ha! I had only been released two days before.

This unfortunately proved to be difficult since all the beds in the hospital were occupied. I sat in the waiting room with my wife, breathing with great difficulty and waiting. It seemed like forever and after sitting, waiting, till late afternoon, it was decided to send me to another hospital where the blood clot could be considered.

My wife drove me to the second hospital, by which time the traffic was at peak level. The drive for me was painful, but we reached the destination without any mishaps.

During the second stay in hospital, my blood was thinned using warfarin, and because the dosage had to be carefully administered and controlled, I was in hospital for *nine* more days.

Nine days! Every day, blood was taken to test the warfarin levels, and every day, a nurse would attend my wound. All this because of one little cough!

Once again, the nursing staff was great. It was a little harder on my wife, though, since the hospital was further from home. She came in each day but not at night. There were always visitors during the evening, so she didn't feel obligated to come in the evening as well, and I insisted that she didn't come.

I encountered no further drama during my stay in hospital. I endured the nine-day stay until they got the warfarin levels correct and the pain had subsided. Warfarin has the same active ingredients as rat killer, so its levels had to be carefully controlled.

Most of the time while in the hospital, I walked along the corridors, read books, or watched TV. The food was great, and I was visited by a doctor each day and was constantly monitored by the nursing staff. There wasn't time for boredom. Besides, I was in the place I had to be at that time. If I had stayed home, I believe my fate might have been very different.

Although I wished that I was at home with my wife, there was no point in being upset because I was in hospital. I didn't brood over my fate. There was no need to cause problems for others, and besides, I didn't want to upset my wife. I was where I needed to be at that moment.

On the last day of my stay in hospital, the doctor arranged to have the catheter removed. That was no problem. I had time to psych myself up to endure the pain that I perceived would follow from its removal.

Friends had told me that the removal of the catheter would be painful. "Like peeing razor blades," one said. "If they don't let down the balloon, you'll go through hell," said another. You can imagine the images I had built up for this process. Imagine also the anxiety I put myself through.

Early next morning, at six o'clock, a nurse came to remove the catheter. "No. It's not ten o'clock yet. I was told ten o'clock," I pleaded frantically as my heartbeat elevated and panic set in.

"Don't forget to let the balloon down," I said knowingly and with as much dignity as I could muster. "Wait a minute, let me get my breathing right, I'm too anxious." The nurse must have thought I was an idiot! I lay on the bed with my PJ "dacks" down around my ankles, sweating and breathing heavily.

Anyway, I tried to regulate my breathing, closed my eyes, and waited. All I felt was a slight tension as the catheter tube was removed. Imagine my relief! No pain. Fantastic!

I dressed and sat in bed wondering what it would be like when I went to the toilet. Would it be like peeing razor blades? I waited until I couldn't hold on any longer and just had to go to relieve myself and guess what! No pain. Yes, the urine flowed very fast since the urethra had been expanded from having the catheter, but no pain. The myths had been dispelled, and when I told the sooth-sayers, they held onto their story.

Was it possible that since the catheter was in for about three weeks that the expanded urethra allowed it to be removed more easily? My friends only had the catheter for two days, so resistance may have been met, producing the sensations they described.

PS: My brother experienced discomfort when he had his catheter removed. He also encountered other problems that he was told occur statistically in about 50 percent of males. When the catheter was removed and he practiced the pelvic floor exercises taught for bladder control, he found that his urine flow slowed to zero, which caused him a lot of pain since he couldn't relieve himself. He doubled over in agony with a full bladder that he couldn't empty.

He returned to hospital to have a catheter inserted to gain relief. He also had to learn how to insert the catheter himself, since he had to do this once a day for the next week. If he didn't insert the catheter, then he couldn't urinate.

One week later, his situation was reassessed. It was decided to insert a catheter with the bag for a two-week period, something to do with relaxing the muscles that controlled the bladder. Apparently my brother had strong sphincter muscles that closed off his bladder, and he couldn't relax the muscle no matter how hard he tried.

Fortunately after the second insertion of the catheter, once it was removed, he encountered no more difficulty. He did, however, experience discomfort with the catheter but managed to endure it. It is now a distant memory and he is clear of cancer.

So What Did I Learn?

Don't lie to your doctor! It may cause complications that are entirely unnecessary. I was lucky, but if the clot had moved to the brain instead

Ian Newbegin

of the lung, or if the nurse hadn't recognised the symptoms, my circumstances may have been different.

What I went through after the operation was entirely my fault and could have been avoided. I didn't have to have an ugly scar across my abdomen, but because of my stupid actions, I suffered the consequences.

Hospitals are places of caring, and the nursing staff worked hard to look after my interests. I can't speak more highly about the quality of care I received at both hospitals and by the visiting nurses. I never encountered a grouchy nurse, though I can imagine them coming across a few irritable patients. In fact, all hospital staff were very considerate of my privacy, and I have to admit that the food was great.

I didn't let my thoughts dwell on the operation, so I didn't suffer any ill feelings or mood swings because of my thoughts. In fact, after the operation, I rarely thought about what had happened. I looked to the future and wondered when I'd return to work. Fancy that! I wanted to get back to work.

The operation produced nowhere near the amount of pain I imagined, and after the event, I have no regrets. In my opinion, I was cancer free and free to live a normal life.

40

Post-Operative Meetings

After returning home from my second stay in hospital, I had to meet with the urologist weekly at first, then every three months, and finally, every six months. At least this was the plan. A PSA test preceded each visit, and the levels were expected to be reduced to zero if everything had gone well.

My first PSA level was 0.2, not significant but accountable. The specialist explained that the level may have been due to residual prostate tissue remaining after the operation, but, he assured me it should reduce to zero as the tissue died. Made sense to me, so why worry?

However, the levels didn't decrease. In fact, the levels *increased* with time. This suggested *something else*. The specialist reminded me that one of the cancer clusters was on the margin and may have been attached to tissue at the site of the prostate bed. Watchful waiting was on the agenda now.

During this time, I felt great. There were no ill effects, and I was able to work as if I hadn't needed the operation. In other words, everything returned to normal in my life, except that I still had to have blood tests to monitor the PSA levels. And yes, gentlemen, sexual relations can carry on with an extremely different feeling during the climax. It was like "the agony and the ecstasy" all rolled in together.

The Cancer Returns

Three years passed, and the PSA level continued to increase slowly, ultimately to 0.7.

Now this level was not detrimental to my health but suggested to the specialist that cancerous cells could be growing and might be problematic later. At this stage, the cells couldn't be detected since the cluster was very small; the only indicator for its existence was the PSA levels in my blood.

"I have reason to believe that there may be cancer cells growing at the site of the prostate bed. I've checked the original CT scan and have shown the images to a colleague for verification. Together, we believe that the cancer is still contained," the specialist explained, much to my annoyance—not at the containment, but the fact that I still had cancer.

Ah yes, that bloody word again. Cancer! This time I was a lot more accepting of the situation, as was my wife. It couldn't be measured and was contained. It hadn't metastasized and spread throughout my body, which was a possible scenario, given that the cancer was on the margin of the prostate.

So what now?

I still had cancer, albeit an immeasurable amount! But how do you trust this stuff?

Even though I accepted what the specialist had told me, I still imagined my body with cancer and couldn't deny the fact that it might spread throughout my body, radiating its tentacles into every nook and cranny, or so my childhood fantasy went. It was time to be positive about the disease again.

The specialist explained that unlike other cancers, particularly skin cancer, this cancer would be slow growing, and if removed now, then the chances for it to metastasize would be reduced.

Remove it now! How could this be done?

Surgery was not an option.

Watchful waiting was certainly an option, but it had run its course. This process involved continued measurement of PSA levels until when, or if, they reached an unsatisfactory level; action would then need to be taken.

Fortunately for me, my specialist thought that I had already reached an unacceptable level, and since he thought that the cancer was contained, the best option would be to have radiotherapy—now. The PSA level was only at 0.7, but given that it had increased in three months and the last increase was the biggest increase (0.5 to 0.7), there was reason for concern.

Once again, the specialist gave me options with my wife present. Once again, we reached our decision before the end of the meeting.

"I would like you to have the radiotherapy and hormone therapy at the same time. This will give us the greatest change to eliminate the cancer," he said as we listened enthusiastically, waiting for the "however."

"You can have radiotherapy alone, but if any cells become resistant to the treatment, with time, they will grow and an alternative treatment will be required," the specialist explained.

Aha! I get that, I thought.

"The hormone treatment doesn't work to kill the cancer cells but to limit their growth, often stopping it," he added.

This sounded promising. Since the growth of the cancer cells was slow and only detectable by PSA levels, it seemed logical to proceed with the treatment as outlined. The radiotherapy would destroy most, if not all, of the cancer cells, and the hormone therapy would slow or stop the growth of any remaining cells.

Of course, the cells could become resistant to the hormone treatment too, but the odds were certainly improving. Doing nothing was not an option.

I made an appointment see a radiation oncologist, who incidentally was the surgeon my specialist consulted earlier.

I met with the radiation oncologist, and he explained the process. The treatment would last for seven weeks, and I would need to attend the radiotherapy unit each week day for the seven-week period, meeting with him once a week to discuss the progress of the treatment.

At the same time, I would begin the hormone treatment that would last for two years and that consisted of taking an Androcur tablet daily immediately after a meal and having a hormone implant inserted just below the skin of my abdomen every three months. The treatment was described in brief earlier, but now that I had to endure the treatment, it was important for me to understand the consequences of the treatment, and these findings are provided for you below.

Androcur contains cyproterone acetate, an antiandrogen that *blocks the action* of the androgen, testosterone, while the LHRH (Zoladex) insert *prevents the production* of testosterone.

Chemical castration!

The same effect could have been achieved if I had been castrated. The LHRH, or Zoladex, prevents testosterone from being produced during the time that the implant is inserted. No more amorous moments, no partial erections; I was entering male menopause, hot flashes and all.

Happily, Androcur prevents hot flashes but had its own problems. Liver failure was a possibility, a small possibility, but nevertheless, a chance. So too was memory loss, which could lead to another dreaded disorder, Alzheimer's.

"The chances for contracting Alzheimer's is very remote," I was told, but still, it was a chance.

Enduring menopause also meant that I might suffer mood swings or depression. This was a small price to pay if the cancer was going to be eliminated. Over the two-year period, I experienced mood swings and suffered low levels of depression, which I endured rather than taking pills. I also suffered memory loss, but it is under control now.

PS: My depression got worse with time. After completing the hormone treatment (two years later), my depression levels elevated. I have included a description of depression below since it is another disorder that many males do not want to talk about and that you may need to consider. Depression is a common disorder that is *often experienced* after a chronic illness.

It is important that you fully understand the consequences of the treatment taken. Ask questions. Don't leave anything to chance. Yes, there may be side effects if you have medication, and you should be aware of them too or you may worry unnecessarily.

Radiotherapy

Before the radiotherapy treatment could start, the target site had to be accurately mapped, so I was sent to have another CT scan. During this time, I was marked with permanent ink so my body could be aligned correctly during the treatment. The markings were so small that only the trained eye could see them, keeping my anti-tattoo attitude intact.

A week before treatment, I had to administer an enema suppository each night to help establish a constant target size. The enema also had to be administered during treatment *if* I encountered difficulty using my bowels during the day.

Day one of my treatment had me filling out preferred times for the treatment, which were written on an appointment card for a two-week period, along with the doctor's appointments. I chose early morning because I planned on going to work after the treatment. Since I lived forty kilometres from the hospital and work was close to the hospital, late treatment times would mean hanging around and travelling in peak traffic.

Each morning I attended the radiotherapy unit for treatment, which consisted of a series of x-rays being fired into the site from three different directions using a linear accelerator. Firing x-rays from three directions ensured that damage could be minimised around the surrounding tissue. Only the target area received the *full dose* of radiation, which consisted of the *sum of each* radiation fired during each daily session.

On each visit, I would lie on a hydraulically operated table, which could be manoeuvred into position for radiation once I was positioned correctly on the table. The device would rotate in a vertical circle around my body, stopping at the three target positions to fire the x-rays.

Five weeks into the treatment, and it changed. The target area had reduced in size, so the x-rays were concentrated onto a smaller region. Overall, I received seventy Gray (two Gray per day) of x-ray, the last twenty units being concentrated at the *smaller* target site. The amount of x-rays received per patient depends on the body mass and amount of tissue to be penetrated, and the dosage was calculated by computer.

I met many people while waiting for my treatment. One man was being scanned for a brain tumour and another woman for breast cancer. The linear accelerator, or radiation device, is used to target many types of cancer, each cancer varying in body location and size.

So that only the target region received the correct dosage, a *focussing* device was put in the path of the radiation, ensuring that the target area was kept to a minimum, thus protecting the surrounding tissue.

Imagine if a dam burst and all the water spread over the land below. There would be devastation, but if the water was allowed to pass through a spillway that directed the water to a specific location, then the surrounding land would be safe. The targeting device acts like this.

As can be expected, the technicians and nurses were very supportive. If *you* need radiation treatment, and if you ask, they will explain what is happening. I found that the staff was very willing to explain what was being done. When you understand what is happening to you, the ordeal is not as traumatic.

On each day of my visit, the technicians made sure I didn't move during the treatment, reminding me on each occasion as they took the necessary time to line my body up with the device so that only the target area received the required radiation. It is important while being radiated that movement is limited. You can't even yawn!

By the way, you feel nothing during the process. It is painless.

My diet had necessarily changed for the period of treatment and for three weeks after the treatment. Essentially *fibre*, which consisted of food that could not be completely digested, was *removed* from the diet. A diet sheet was given to me by the doctor and the nursing staff, thus ensuring that I knew what food I should consume.

For my situation, because the radiation area was the site of the prostate, it meant that radiation had to pass through my intestines. Consequently, it was important for me to stick to the diet, since the bowel motions could have changed during the treatment. If the motions become restricted, then the high fibre might make it difficult to pass stools. Also, high fibre could cause *aggravation* within the bowel *because of* the radiation. I certainly didn't want any problems, so I stuck to the diet.

I remained on the diet for a period of ten weeks and suffered no ill effects. I had loose bowels for a short period as well as difficult moments in passing stools, but on the whole, I didn't suffer. Yes, I might have felt a little tenderness around the radiation sites, something like sunburn, but that was the extent of it.

A nurse was on duty each day at the radiotherapy unit, so if any ill effects appeared, or if I had any concerns about the treatment, my needs could be immediately considered.

The weekly doctor's appointment also gave me the opportunity to ask questions about the treatment and for the doctor to determine whether the procedure was proceeding satisfactorily. Happily, my treatment seemed to be going to plan, though its overall effectiveness couldn't be determined until post-procedural tests were performed. Two weeks after the treatment, I met with the radiation oncologist.

If you need to have radiation treatment, don't fear it. If you follow the instructions given by the nursing staff and doctor, there is no reason to believe that you will feel any ill effects. Whether or not you go to work is entirely up to you and your doctor. Tiredness is often a side effect of the radiation, so driving or using heavy equipment might be a limiting factor.

Hormone Treatment Explained

The male sex hormone, testosterone (an androgen), is known to promote the growth of cancer cells located within the prostate. Therefore, in the early days of treating prostate cancer, removal of the testes was a real option since they are responsible for producing testosterone.

Happily, this process (orchidectomy) is no longer performed; the same effect can be produced by using pharmaceutical products such as

Zolodex (Goselerin), effectively resulting in chemical castration *if the treatment is maintained.*

In broad, simplistic detail, consider the following explanation of how testosterone is produced.

- Hypothalamus (located in centre of the brain) releases

- Gonadotrophin releasing hormone (GnRH), which stimulates

- Pituitary gland to release

- Leutinising hormone (LH), which stimulates

- Testes to produce testosterone.

Under normal circumstances, testosterone is essential for a male's development (during puberty) and for the production of sperm. The system alluded to above has a feedback mechanism that slows the production of testosterone when production is high and increases the production when the level of testosterone is low.

However, when cancer cells are present, testosterone stimulates the growth of these cells, particularly when the cancer initiates in the prostate.

Zolodex, or similar agents, is injected under the skin where the active ingredient is slowly released into the body over a period of time (for me, three months). Zolodex acts on the *antagonist* to GnRH and testosterone, thereby *preventing* the testes from producing testosterone.

If any prostate cancer cells remain in the body after the initial treatment, Zolodex can stop their growth. It *does not* destroy the cancer.

The side effects of such treatment are similar to those of menopause and include: *hot flashes, loss of sexual potency and drive, mood swings, insomnia, loss of strength, fatigue, loss of body hair, and cognitive changes.* These are the common side effects and may or may not occur together. I, for instance, didn't experience loss of strength or fatigue until after one and one half years, though I did experience hair loss on my arms and legs.

Hormone treatment is usually performed at the same time as radiation therapy to help shrink the prostate, should this be the initial treatment and therefore, the target radiation site.

After two years of hormone therapy, my secondary treatment, I developed memory problems and became short tempered. Memory loss was a major concern for me, since all I could visualise was myself with Alzheimer's disease. "Not so," said the doctor. "Thank you," said I.

Now that I was free of any form of treatment, I could expect an improvement in my general feeling of well being, though I still felt very tired, and despite the doctor's assurance about memory, I was still forgetful. Ah well, I supposed I needed to give the whole process time.

My knees became very hairy, and hair growth on my arms returned but not my legs. My daughter commented about my dirty knees and went into hysterics when she saw that the dirt was hair.

I was suffering from a *consequence* of the hormone treatment, not a side effect. Zolodex certainly reduced the amount of testosterone being produced, keeping the growth of the cancer in check. Unfortunately, *reduction* in testosterone levels that normally occurs in men as we age, hopefully at a late age, can affect memory. Have I told you about my forgetfulness?

Since I had come off the hormone treatment, I could expect my testosterone levels to increase and with it, a return of memory. At the time of writing this book, my testosterone levels were very low. I also suffered depression (described later) and anxiety during the latter stages of the treatment, but *knowing that the treatment was the cause*, I am not overly concerned. Yet!

A Diversion—Alternative Treatments

I need to come clean at this point about my treatment. Yes, it did proceed basically as the description offered above, but when I first learnt that the cancer was still present, *before* I started the radiotherapy, I looked for alternative treatments.

Three months before the blood test that suggested to the urologist and oncologist that I needed radio therapy, I read up on alternative, natural treatments.

Now I cannot say categorically that such treatments do not work, but I can say they didn't work for me within the time frame I allowed.

My logic was to use the blood test as the determinant for the effectiveness of the alternative treatment, which involved ingesting *apricot kernels*, which incidentally tasted like bitter almonds. I ground the kernels and sprinkled them over my cereal.

I bought the kernels over the Internet and read widely about their healing powers. The more I read, the more I was convinced that I should try it. Ah, the power of the Internet. Don't believe everything you read over the net.

It was suggested that apricot kernels, which contain low levels of cyanide, would destroy the cancer cells. The reckoning behind this theory relies on the suggestion that cyanide would be more readily taken up by the *more active and faster growing* cancer cells, thus increasing in concentration over a period of time, and therefore, destroying the cancer cells before damage could be inflicted on normal cells.

Cyanide is a poison and destroys body cells, but taken in small doses such as that in a dozen or so apricot kernels taken daily, it can be taken up by the cancer cells, and when it reaches the desired concentration, destroy the cells. The idea here, of course, is to use the fact that cancer cells are more active than normal cells and will absorb most of the cyanide.

Who do you believe? Another source of information about ingesting apricot kernels suggested that vitamin B17, which is also known as laetrile or amygdalin, were the active ingredients. Whatever the active ingredient may be, it is possible that I didn't take it correctly, and maybe my diet should have changed during the treatment time. I wasn't told, so I ate my normal meals.

I didn't tell my doctor about my little excursion. The admission comes now.

Hey! I felt great during this time of indulgence. I really believed that I had *something else to pin my hopes on,* and I made certain that I took the required dosage of freshly ground kernels each day.

My sole monitoring process was the impending blood test. If ingesting apricot kernels had worked, then I could expect to find a corresponding decrease in PSA level. Testimonials endorsing the idea suggested that results would be seen within weeks of taking the kernels in the appropriate dosage.

Not so.

My next blood test indicated an increase in PSA level, *and it was the biggest increase to date.*

There's more to this saga.

One month before the above-mentioned blood test, someone suggested that I try Essiac (Caisse backwards) tea, a herb mix formulated by a native Ojibwa medicine man in Canada who passed the formula onto a nurse, Rene Caisse, who nursed cancer patients and who noticed that the herb mix cured patients of cancer. It too was supposed to produce miracles, and I thought, coupled with the apricot kernels, I must've been onto a winner.

Imagine how I felt taking a double whammy of natural ingredients, both of which, it was claimed, would cure me of cancer. I couldn't lose; surely one of them would work!

At least it cured me of looking for alternative treatments.

I am no expert, and maybe I didn't give the process enough time. However, there's enough pessimist in me to suggest that the treatments were never going to work. *Be guided by your doctor.* They at least have had training in their reported area of expertise.

The advice given to me was provided by well-meaning friends and via the Internet, *not* trained herbologists. This too could have been a fault in my small experiment. A herbologist might have been able to control the dosage or direct me towards a product that worked. I don't know. I didn't bother to find out, and neither did I want to.

It's also quite possible that the herb could have interfered with the doctor's treatment, causing dire consequences. Consider the following example; I was on Zoloft (a serotonin reuptake inhibitor) for the control of depression. I was told that the herb St. Johns wort would work just as well and without the side effects of Zoloft. I didn't want to just take the herb, so I researched it over the Internet and through a doctor. If I had taken the herb while taking Zoloft, it was quite possible that I would have suffered from serotonin syndrome, meaning a build up of the very hormone that was being inhibited by Zoloft. Isn't this good enough reason to consult a doctor?

If you are seeking an alternative treatment, consult your doctor first. Let him or her know what you intend to ingest so that their monitoring system includes whatever else you might do. It is possible that my alternative treatment may have ultimately changed the course of action taken, but I didn't take my own advice. I told no one.

Now That It's Over

Post-Radiotherapy Treatment

I met with the radiation oncologist two weeks after the treatment had finished. I hadn't had any blood tests, so I wondered what would be discussed since he couldn't tell me anything about the PSA levels or whether the treatment had worked.

We discussed my well being. He asked questions about my mental health, bowel movements, and urine issues. Since I had no real problems, the meeting finished with the instruction to have a blood test six weeks after the treatment finishing time, and I was told to stop taking the Androcur tablets.

I took Androcur for a period of ten weeks, during which time it prevented hot flashes but its prime purpose was to stop the *action* of testosterone until the Zolodex implant took effect.

"We need to give time for any residual PSA to be eliminated or at least to stabilise," the radiation oncologist told me. Now at least I knew why I wasn't asked to have a blood test before visiting the oncologist after the treatment had finished.

Four weeks later, I went for a blood test.

This time, however, I met with the urologist, and the results of the blood tests were also forwarded to the radiation oncologist. I was put on a roster to see either the urologist or oncologist in turn so that a predetermined time passed while being monitored. The result of my meeting with one of the specialists was passed onto the other. Both needed to keep track of what was going on, and by rotating the appointments, this was assured.

"The PSA levels cannot be measured with certainty," he told me.

I was elated. *It's gone,* I thought.

"This is what we were aiming for; however, it doesn't mean that we have eliminated the cancer."

Instant deflation.

"We're sure that we have targeted the correct area and have eliminated most of the cancer, but we can't be certain. The hormone treatment should keep the growth rate of any remaining cells at a low level."

Feeling better.

"I want to see you in six months time, and if the count remains immeasurable, I won't need to see you till twelve months after." He smiled and then wrote out a script for the next blood test.

Of course he couldn't say that the cancer had been eliminated! *Nothing is certain.* However, as far as I was concerned, the cancer had been eliminated, and I was going to live life as if it wasn't present.

All I had to endure now was the hormone treatment. As I indicated earlier, after two years of hormone treatment, I have not felt any ill effects with the exception of anxiety attacks, low-level depression, hot flashes, and the occasional feeling of exhaustion. Since I was aware of these side effects, they haven't produced any lasting changes to my life. Yes, I might be moodier and feel down every now and then, but it's under control. I'd rather endure the side effects than suffer the prospect that the cancer might continue to grow at its previous level. My only hope at this time is that my memory will return to normal.

PS: I wrote this paragraph two years after completing the hormone treatment. Yes, I still suffer from depression, but the hotflashes have reduced. Unfortunately, a new problem has shown itself. A side effect of the hormone treatment is osteoporosis. It doesn't occur in many males, but I contracted a lesser form of the disorder called osteopaenia, a brittle bone disorder that requires me to take calcium tablets.

I am not unduly worried by this, but it means that I need to change my lifestyle a little. I found out that I had the disorder when I went to see my doctor because of a severe pain I felt in my back. It felt like someone had punched me square in the middle of my back. It hurt when I breathed but subsided with time during the day. A vertebra had collapsed as a result of osteopaenia. Ah well! At least it could be treated quite simply—a pill a day and I have to watch what I do physically. I used to do sit-ups but had to stop due to the collapsed vertebra.

So Where to Now?

Watchful waiting is on the agenda again. My assumption is that the cancer has been eliminated and as I said above, I plan on living my life accordingly.

I believe in the power of positive thinking even though in my work life I may not have fully lived up to this belief. Regarding the cancer, however, my plan is to revisit the practice of tai chi where I can learn to relax and maintain my positive thinking. I also believe that this practice will help my depression and anxiety.

At this stage, I will end my personal encounter with cancer of the prostate and write more formally about cancer and its treatment. My experience was very real, and the outcome could quite easily have resulted in further sickness. I may have been saved from dying earlier than I would have liked, but I cannot be complacent about the disease. Neither can you. If you suspect anything negative about your health, see your family doctor.

PPS: You wouldn't believe it! It is three years after the hormone treatment (2010), and the cancer has returned, with the indicating PSA level being 6.6, the highest since the operation. I am back on hormones with hot flashes and lack of sleep. My depression rose during the ensuring period, and I am being treated for it too. If the PSA level does not decrease, I will be given a new alternative treatment, a treatment I know nothing about. Ah well!

Ah well indeed. I am pleased to announce that as of 2011, the PSA level has dropped to 0.5, but there is a consequence to this, I will need to stay on the hormone treatment until … I don't know when. But I am enjoying life.

Attitude

A person's attitude towards life is a factor worth considering during any illness. An individual can be pessimistic or optimistic, depressed or not, anxious, suffer low self-esteem, or be going through divorce or grieving over a loved one, yet through each of these instances or combinations of instances, the person *can maintain* a positive outlook on life.

This is not an "It won't happen to me" attitude towards life but a healthy look at one's place in the middle of all the trauma or bad things happening around us. Even a pessimist can argue that cancer will not take his or her life, albeit with much "toing" and "froing," but cancer can be defeated.

Consider the following hypothetical pessimistic self-talk.

"I've got cancer, I'll die for sure. No, wait a minute, I've a good family and still have a lot more to give, so why should this cancer take my life? Yeah, but families don't cure cancer. What about Freddy? He died from cancer recently and he was a good man. A good man yes, but he never went to the doctors for a checkup until it was too late."

And so it goes with the pessimist until he/she convinces him or herself that life will go on *for him or her*. I know since I am a pessimist.

When confronting a disease of any kind, it is always healthy to have a positive outlook towards the cure of that disease and life in general. Giving in to the disease destroys life, both physically and emotionally. When we become dependent on others by giving in to our emotions, we lose our lives.

Being dependent on others for support doesn't mean that you surrender your life to the carer. Necessary dependency on others is not a bad thing either, particularly when you need support to maintain the quality of your life. Only when you let the carer make every decision do you surrender your life. Encountering cancer can be like this.

Sustained thinking that the world will end, that you will surely die, is a sure-fire way of letting the cancer take control of your life. Even in the face of adversity, a solution often presents itself.

Consider the story about two frogs (author not known).

Two frogs were hopping around a farm yard when they came across a large, round wooden container. "Let's go and have a look," said one of the frogs. They hopped over to the container and jumped up onto a stool that was near it and finally onto the edge of the container.

It held a white liquid. "I'm hot. Let's jump in for a swim," said one of the frogs.

They jumped in and swam around happily, dunking each other into the liquid and generally frolicked around. They soon tired, "I'm getting tired. Boy, it seems to be getting harder to swim. Let's get out and rest."

"Good idea," the other frog replied, but when they tried to get out, they found that the level of the liquid was too far below the lip of the container. "It's too far. We'll have to frog paddle for a while until someone saves us," said one of the frogs.

They paddled around for a few minutes more but soon wearied. "I'm getting too tired and exhausted. I can't swim anymore."

"Hang on a little longer," the other frog replied, but no, his friend stopped swimming and slowly sank to the bottom.

The surviving frog was distraught. He swam around frantically in grief and slowly, he too found it difficult to swim in this white liquid. In fact, the liquid became solid, and he hopped on to its surface and jumped out, leaving his friend at the bottom of the container.

The moral? Don't give up. A solution will present itself, usually in the form of treatment, but a positive attitude that life will go on will certainly help.

Stress

A body under emotional stress is less likely to respond positively to treatment than a body looking forward to living. Stress often results in a negative attitude and everything this attitude brings with it. Because stress alters the balance of hormones in the body, it is possible that certain treatments may take longer to effect change. Besides, your mind will ensure that the repair process takes longer or doesn't occur because after all, *"I've got cancer and there's nothing that can be done about it."* What a cop out!

Maintain a healthy attitude and you will view your situation through different eyes. Everything is not a lost cause. You can help the healing process, and there is a strong possibility that you will defeat the condition. Self-pity will be your biggest downfall next to bravado. If you continue to think negatively about cancer, if you continue to think doom, then you will be assured of the gloom that follows. "Hey! I'm a man. I'm tough. There's nothing wrong with me. My sex life is great. Nah, I'm okay." These are words only; what happens because of the cancer will not follow this sentiment. Believe me.

Look at the health stories told on television about people in hospital who are suffering from possibly terminal diseases. I am always amazed at how they live in hope of an organ donation or the outcome of the next treatment. The kids in these stories always seem to have a positive outlook. I remember seeing a story on a small boy who was asked what would happen if he didn't have a particular treatment. He said, "I'll die" as he played with his toy car, and then he said, "But the doctors are good, and they'll help me." It broke me up! What did I have to worry about? This kid had a rare disorder (I can't recall what it was), but he played and smiled all through the interview. Fantastic!

Consider the following story. A young girl stood on the side of a pool, bent at the knees, arms backwards and rocking on her feet, trying to get the courage to jump into the water. Her father, who was in the pool, had his arms up ready to catch her. He was shouting, "Come on, darling, Daddy will catch you." The little girl thought about it for a short time, still rocking on her feet, and then she launched herself into her father's arms. She took the plunge and jumped.

Don't be scared to take the plunge. Trust others, and trust yourself. Share your experience with your family; they'll offer unlimited support if you let them. *You are worth it.* Above all, trust your doctor. You can speculate about the state of your prostate, but only the doctor can tell you with any certainty what the state of your prostate truly is.

It's the same for other diseases. Don't listen to stories about a friend of a friend who died. Your doctor will give you hope where hope is required, and with a positive attitude, who knows what the outcome might be. Survival is a certainly a strong possibility.

Let's look at another story. Alice was walking along a path in Wonderland when she came to a fork in the road. *Oh dear, which path should I take?* she thought to herself.

She looked up into a tree and saw a Cheshire cat. "Please, Mr. Cat, can you tell me which path I should take?" she said to the grinning Cheshire cat.

"It depends on where it is you want to go," the cat replied to Alice.

"Oh! I don't know really," she answered.

To which the cat said, "Then it doesn't matter which path you take."

I consider myself to be a pessimist, but I have found that optimism *can be learnt.* Pessimism isn't an innate characteristic; it too is learnt. Nobody is doomed to eternal pessimism because of his or her nature. Thinking may lead towards a pessimistic outcome, but only if we allow the thinking to proceed in its usual manner. I learnt very quickly that cancer of the prostate did not need to claim my life. I didn't want to be a statistic, so I changed the way I viewed the disease, and you know what! It wasn't difficult to do. *Optimism provides hope.*

You have very real choices. Choose the path that is full of hope and support. Be optimistic about the outcome, and chances are, it will be a positive one. What is certain is that not doing anything at all will almost certainly result in ill health or possible death.

How many men have died needlessly because they didn't have a checkup on the state of their prostate? Have you had a checkup? If your urine flow is slow or you have difficulty starting, what do you think about the situation? Have a checkup. It may save your life.

A Friend's Plight

In 2007, a work colleague approached me about cancer of the prostate. He was a little apprehensive and wanted to talk to me because I had undergone a procedure that he was likely to have. He was fifty-five years old.

"I don't know yet," he said when I asked him questions about his prostate. "My prostate was swollen when I had the digital inspection, but the PSA level was normal. My doctor wants me to see a specialist."

I assured him that seeing a specialist was a precautionary action and told him that if any future test results were positive for cancer, then he would be in safe hands. One week later, he went to see a specialist and one week after that, the result of the biopsy was given to him.

"I have three out of six needle point samples with cancer, all within the prostate," he said nervously. "All I want to do is get it out." The specialist told him that there was no need to hurry. The Gleeson score (aggressiveness of the cancer) was six, indicating a moderately aggressive cancer.

I spoke about my experience and the fact that I too wanted the cancer removed. When you first hear about cancer in your body, it is an anxious moment, and my friend, like many others with this insidious disease, only wanted to be rid of it. I mean, the very word cancer conjures up negative images with consequential negative thoughts.

"He (the specialist) is going to use keyhole surgery. I should be back at work within three weeks," he said, telling me that it was going to cost him about five thousand dollars, even though he had private health insurance. A costly exercise, true, but what is the cost of life? With keyhole surgery, he wouldn't have the long, ugly scar that I have.

"I just want it out. The specialist says that the operation can be done later, but I don't want to give it a chance to metastasise," he said.

I understood his feelings. Nobody wants cancer in his or her body. At least with cancer of the prostate, the cancer is localised and any treatment is likely to contain the cancer or eliminate it from the prostate, provided it is recognized early. I don't envy those who have had a cancer spread throughout their bodies and had to suffer chemotherapy. My friend was right to think the way he did.

Happily, he was very positive about his prospects, and I had no doubt that he would come through the ordeal safely. He had teenage children and said he wanted to be around to enjoy grandchildren. Quite a natural thought.

Contrast this account with those of my students above. Here my friend acted promptly on a situation that could have ended differently. His kids will probably see him into old age.

The point about the student accounts is the fact that death, particularly premature death, affects others. Children take it harder than we may think, so consider your loved ones, have the relevant tests to determine the health of your prostate, and have peace of mind. *Your family deserves to have you around.*

By the way, my friend had the operation and was walking around school two weeks later. He hadn't returned to school to work, but he looked great. He suffered no pain from the removal of the catheter and now he can live a happy, healthy, normal life.

One year after his operation, his PSA tests have all had a reading of zero, suggesting that his cancer has been eliminated. Great stuff!

My Cousin Also Got the Disease

I have already stated that if one family member has the disease, then the likelihood of another member of the family having it is higher than that of other males. It doesn't mean that you will get the disease, no. But it makes sense to have a test, doesn't it? Particularly if a family member has it.

My cousin called and told me that he was having his prostate removed because he had contracted cancer. He was positive about its eradication since the needle point count was low. He had a radical prostatectomy in 2008, and since then, he has been told that the cancer has returned, or more likely, it wasn't removed in its entirety during the operation. Can you imagine how he felt?

Yes, he was nervous about his predicament, and I told him about my fight with the return of the cancer. This made him feel better, and as could be expected, he was going to face the disease, again, positively.

What did I tell him? Well, first, he didn't know that my cancer had returned, so his interest was heightened. He wanted to know how I felt both during and after radiation treatment. I told him not to worry about the treatment and that the response to the treatment is dependent on the location and size of the cancer. I felt nothing, not a thing—no ill effects. I also told him that I had hormone treatment, which again had no ill effects, though there were side effects.

He asked, rather gingerly, if the hormone treatment could leave an individual impotent. The answer is yes, but not for everyone. During the treatment, the testosterone levels are reduced, so sex may be out of the question, but after the treatment, the testosterone levels can increase, restoring potency—but not necessarily; this must be stated.

Let's get the sex issue over with. If sex is more important than your family, then don't have the operation. Yes, you may lose the ability to gain a full erection. You might need aids, and yes, you might become impotent, but sex can carry on even with a partial erection, and as I said earlier, the experience is very different.

My cousin was happy with my responses to his questions, and I hope this brief explanation helps you too. Cancer of the prostate is not a death sentence. I had my operation in 2001, and in 2011, I am still alive, albeit with a return of the cancer, but I don't plan on going anywhere. So my advice to you is, be guided by your doctor and family. I have said it before and will say it again, so get used to it: *your family is more important than your perception of your manhood.*

PS: The doctors didn't know where the secondary cancer was located. My cousin had to decide on whether or not to have radiation treatment and decided against it since the cancer site was uncertain. He did, however, have hormone treatment, after which the PSA level fell to zero. A great result!

Another Cousin's Story

I was talking with a cousin recently, and as usual when we age, conversation seems to lead towards, "How's your health?" He told me that he had been having trouble digesting food and was told that the state of his prostate could be a possible cause. Subsequently, he went to have the usual tests. The digital test showed that his prostate was indeed enlarged, but when he had a biopsy, none of the needle point samples contained cancer. He had BPH, or benign prostatic hyperplasia, and had a simple operation to reduce the size of his prostate so that the urine could flow normally. What else was disclosed was the fact that his prostate had nothing to do with his poor digestion. At the time of writing, he was undergoing tests to determine why his digestion had changed.

But isn't it great to hear that he didn't have cancer of the prostate? You may experience problems, but it doesn't need to be doom.

A Statistical Diversion

The following information was extracted from the Cancer Council of Victoria. In fact, I recommend that you visit this site and other sites like it on your computer to read the information provided about the various types of cancers. These sites can be accessed by using your search engine and typing "cancer" as the keyword for the search.

The information provided below is presented to demonstrate the prevalence of this disease. We should never be complacent about cancer, and the statistics highlight the fact that it touches each of us in some way, whether it is a family member or yourself at some stage in life.

The table shows percentage data from *all* cancers for the state of Victoria (CANSTAT: Cancer Council of Victoria, 2006). Please note that non-melanocytic skin cancer is not reported here, but it has been said by a reputable organization in NSW that it is suspected as having a high incidence rate.

They decided to report the number of cases and express this number as a percentage of *all cancers* for both incidence rate and death rate. Note: only the most common types of cancers have been presented here.

Common Types of Cancer by Incidence and Death Rate (2006)

Type	Incidence Male (female)	Percent incidence	Death Male (female)	Percent death
Colon	1071 (1090)	8.2 (10.1)	365 (342)	6.9 (8.0)
Rectum	799 (484)	6.1 (4.4)	220 (160)	4.1 (3.7)
Bowel	1850 (1574)	14.2 (14.5)	585 (502)	11.0 (11.7)
Melanoma	1090 (869)	8.4 (8.0)	176 (85)	3.3 (2.0)
Lung	1472 (837)	11.3 (7.7)	1163 (614)	22.0 (14.4)
Breast	23 (3047)	0.2 (28.2)	2 (685)	0.03 (16.1)
Prostate	3838	29.5	730	13.8
Non-Hodgkin's lymphoma	570 (424)	4.4 (3.9)	187 (190)	3.5 (4.4)
All Malignant tumours	13019 (10791)		5283 (4266)	

It is important to realize for this set of data, *age hasn't been taken into consideration.* The chances of contracting a cancer increases with age.

The figures reported above are raw score data (reported incidences) and *do not reflect* the possibilities of contracting cancer. Don't read the statistics as if it is a foregone conclusion that you may be one of the statistics in the future.

Although not shown here, leukaemia is the leading type of cancer in children up to fourteen years, whereas prostate (male) and breast (female) cancer is prevalent for males and females over twenty-five years.

Note that lung cancer has the highest death rate for males, and although it is not the highest for females following breast cancer, it is the highest death rate for both genders over all of Australia.

According to the data, 29 percent of all deaths are due to cancer (all types), and 17.7 percent of all deaths are due to heart disease (not reported above). If we look at individual cancers, such as prostate cancer and breast cancer, rather than collectively, death due to heart disease has the highest incidence (CANSTAT).

The figures presented reflect the incidences and death rate for the year 2006. When you consider the population of Victoria to be over three million, 3,838 cases of prostate cancer may seem small, but this figure (or close to it) *is occurring every year,* and we each have about the same likelihood for contracting the disease, with the chances increasing with age.

It is interesting to note that after reading figures from other states in Australia and other western countries around the world that *similar figures* are generated and the same types of cancer are the main causes of death

Technical Talk

How Does Cancer Develop?

The human body can be loosely compared to a large corporation where each department works in unison with other departments. Imagine if one department became sloppy with its procedures. Its sloppiness would affect those departments that immediately depend on it and would soon affect the whole business, possibly causing it to close. A company that has all departments functioning as they should would be productive. In a healthy organisation, the various departments would communicate between each other and adjust their input or output accordingly.

A healthy human body consists of a myriad of cells all working together to ensure the survival of the body. Energy is not wasted on cell division (producing new cells) unless it is necessary; such is the nature of the body, all cells working in unison.

Not only do cells work together to ensure the health of the individual, but there is also a large variety of cell types that have different functions than other cells in the body so it can function as it was designed to do. For instance, kidney cells are quite different from muscle cells or brain cells and a group of similar cells form, for example, what we call the kidney, each cell functioning to support the operation of the kidney, which is a vital component of the body as a whole. If the kidney fails and nothing is done about it, then, like an ailing business, the body will die.

Early in the growth cycle of a human being, the embryo consists of undifferentiated *stem cells*. As the embryo grows, the stem cells begin to *differentiate* and become cells with a particular function, like an organ, such as kidney cells or brain cells. At first cell division is prolific while the new human grows, eventually reaching a stage where cell division slows down or is even halted.

When we accidently cut ourselves, resting cells get the signal to undergo rapid cell division until the injured site is repaired. This is important when a prostatectomy, or any operation, is performed since an incision is made down the abdomen that must be repaired in quick time to avoid possible infection.

Whenever stem cells divide, one of the two daughter cells remains a stem cell while the other differentiates. So, during our lifetime, we have instances of cell division, proliferation, and cell differentiation, all of which are under the control of specialist proteins in the body, which ensure that the body develops as it should.

Cancer develops when cell division goes wrong. Unlike normal body cells, cancer cells rarely differentiate (and therefore can resemble stem cells) and undergo rapid division, thereby producing a cluster of undifferentiated cells that we call a tumour.

So Why Do Healthy Cells Go Astray?

The root cause of cancer is when certain *genes* within the nucleus a cell, or group of cells, mutate to become *oncogenes* or genes that will cause a cancer by causing the cell to grow *rapidly* and to remain *undifferentiated*.

Gene mutation may result from a number of factors, which can be put into one of two categories:

- Environmental

- Hereditary

Environmental factors include things like chemicals, radiation, and lifestyle. For instance, certain work environments deal with chemicals (carcinogens) that can cause cancer and over a long time period, may result in cancer. Similarly, we may ingest chemicals in our food as additives that over time may cause a cancer. The carcinogen usually causes a mutation in particular genes, resulting in oncogenes and consequently, cancer.

When cancer forms in this way, it is not inherited, since it has resulted from mutating body cells that were affected by a carcinogen.

However, when genes in sex cells (sperm, egg) mutate, the mutated gene will be passed on to the carrier's offspring, which may result in a cancer later in the life of the individual and is usually a specific form of cancer.

Lifestyle and culture may result in an apparent increase in cancer or indeed, an apparent decrease or absence of a cancer. Usually, the food we eat causes this phenomenon, along with the absence or presence of stress.

Cancers, therefore, can be considered as *generalised* or *specific*. Cancers resulting from a carcinogen usually result in a generalised form of cancer initiating in any part of the body. Cancer of the prostate results from cells of the prostate becoming cancerous and is therefore a specific form of cancer. It has been suggested that diet and lifestyle are the main causes of cancer of the prostate, but this is still uncertain. It is also possible that the cancer is inherited and is passed through the family line.

Remember, my brother and cousin also contracted cancer of the prostate, and the chance of my other brother also having the disease must therefore be greater than if neither of his brothers had the disease. It has been reported that if cancer has a history within a family, then the *likelihood* of a member of the family contracting the disease is higher than that of an outsider.

Research also shows that if incidents of breast and ovarian cancer are prevalent within a family, then the males are likely, though they may not, to contract cancer of the prostate. You see, they share a common gene that has been identified, and the gene causes the cancer. Do you have a sister or mother who has had breast or ovarian cancer? My sister had ovarian cancer, and a cousin had cervical cancer, so the research rang true for me, my brother, and my cousin. Don't risk it; get checked by your doctor.

Let's look at healthy cells again for the moment.

Healthy cells are bound (held) together by collagen and other binding substrates. They don't use any more energy than is necessary for survival with the cell wall dictating how much nutrition is taken into the cell. Finally, a healthy cell will not divide to produce a new cell unless the appropriate signal is given.

So what about a cancer cell? The binding substrate is *loosely* binding with cancer cells; hence they may break away from a cluster and migrate to another site to grow. This is called metastasis.

The cell walls of cancer cells also allow more nutrients to enter the cell than would otherwise be the case. With this extra energy, a cancer cell can grow and undergo cell division, thus causing a proliferation of large, undifferentiated cells, which is the tumour.

There are other factors contributing to cancer growth and its development, but what is presented here is sufficient to help you to understand how cancer forms. My hope is that the mystery behind what is called cancer has been dispersed.

Angiogenesis

All cells require nutrients and oxygen for growth, both of which get to the cell through blood vessels. Under normal conditions, cell growth results in a healthy individual built from a variety of cells working in unison to ensure the survival of the individual.

When cancer develops, to ensure an ample supply of nutrients and oxygen, the cancer cells produce a protein called vascular endothelial growth factor (VEGF), which promotes the growth of blood vessels from the local area within the growing tumour.

In this way, a group of cancer cells grow to become a tumour with an ample supply of blood vessels that are capable of supplying the necessary nutrients and oxygen to sustain its growth. The process where cancer cells cause the growth of blood vessels through the cancerous clump is called *angiogenesis*.

It stands to reason that the removal of a cancerous growth early in its growth cycle is more likely to result in an improved lifestyle for the individual if the removal occurs before the clump under goes angiogenesis.

Consider the recurrence of cancer after the removal of the prostate. Raised PSA levels are the usual indicators for the doctor to suggest that cancerous prostate cells still exist. In my case, the cells couldn't be seen and were surmised to be present and assumed to be located at the site of the deceased prostate. Minimising the possibility of angiogenesis by radiating the site where the prostate was located has thus far prevented the continued growth of the cancer. If the cancer had gone undetected, there is a strong possibility that the cells may have grown into a tumour with its own blood supply or metastasised, spreading to other areas in the body.

Grading and Staging of Cancer of the Prostate

The word cancer conjures up images of gloom and doom. To help you understand that having cancer of the prostate does not necessarily mean you will die from the disease, the *grading* of the cancer is described below. The most common grading system used is the *Gleason* score system.

After a biopsy, the two most common patterns of cells (compared to normal cells) are scored and added together, resulting in a Gleason score from two to ten.

A low score (four or less) suggests that the cells most resemble normal cells and are the least dangerous.

An intermediate score (four to seven) suggests that the cells are moderately differentiated, resulting in a low- to moderate-grade cancer. High PSA may also confirm this grade.

A high score (greater than eight) occurs when the cells least resemble normal cells. They are very aggressive and fast growing and often invade other areas. Such cancers are hard to treat.

Your doctor will tell you the Gleason score after a biopsy and explain what it means to you. What is important here is for you to understand that the different grades provide different options and offers hope when discussing the disease, which only seems to offer doom. Let your doctor interpret the Gleason score for you. He or she will be able to give you the best prospect. What I have offered above is a rough guide. Doctors do not work on rough guides.

Staging of the cancer describes how much and where the cancer is located. Stages A and B find the cancer within the prostate and are determined by high PSA (stage A) and a digital inspection (stage B). A stage C cancer occurs when the cancer is found outside of the prostate and stage D when it has spread to the lymph nodes or bones.

The grade and stage of the cancer, when classified, affect one's long-term chances for survival. You can elect to not know the grade or stage if you want and take each day in turn. This attitude may help you to overcome the cancer, particularly if you adopt a positive attitude.

For my part, I wanted to know the grade (six) and the stage (B) since I now had something on which I could focus with the aim of eliminating the disease from my body.

Has it gone? Time will be the telling factor.

Healthy Eating

Food has long been accepted, or rejected, for its nutritional value. In some cultures, food has been noted for its medicinal purposes, evident in the Western world with the rising numbers of herbalists. Improved scientific methods have enhanced our understanding of both the nutritional and medicinal aspects of food. Some experts have gone as far as to say which foods are good at preventing diseases—including cancer.

Doctors prescribe medicines to help control the growth of cancer. The medicine is usually prescribed *after* the event—that is, after an individual has been diagnosed with cancer. Scientists have shown that certain vegetables and fruits have enzymes that can *prevent* cancer (statistical evidence only) and that limit the growth of a cancer by preventing angiogenesis.

Such enzymes are called *phytochemicals* and are responsible for the colour, odour, and taste of the vegetable or fruit. Tomatoes, the cabbage family, and garlic are some plants listed as having high phytochemical content.

It is important to note that the term *phytochemical* is a generic name; the actual *family* name is dependent on the plant type, for instance, delphinidin in blueberries, lycopene in tomatoes, and sulphoraphane in broccoli. With regard to prostate cancer, *tomatoes and green tea* are often mentioned as good foods for its prevention.

Diet books are abundant in our society, so books about food are not unfamiliar to us. There are books about antioxidants and a whole range of diets, so it shouldn't be surprising to learn that there are books about food and their ability to prevent cancer. It doesn't hurt an individual to know about foods and their healing powers, but if you suspect cancer or are suffering an unknown illness, it is always best to consult your doctor.

An easy to read book about food and cancer is *Foods that Fight Cancer* by Richard Beliveau and Denis Gingras.

The Prostate

After all that has been written so far, we finally get to ask, what is this organ called the prostate? It is a male-only organ located just in front of the bowel and below the bladder and is about the size of a walnut, hence the cover, though very much softer than a walnut. The prostate surrounds part of the urethra, a tube coming from the bladder exiting at the penis and that is the pathway for both urine and sperm to exit the body.

It is approximately 30 percent muscle, the rest of the prostate consisting of glandular tissue, which is responsible for producing part of the seminal fluid. The prostate releases seminal fluid (semen) into the urethra during sexual intercourse, which mixes with the sperm produced in the testes. Semen has two functions: it protects the sperm from the acid environment it will find when it enters the uterus of the female partner, and it has nutrients for the sperm, thus extending its otherwise short life.

The prostate also has nerve cells attached to it that stimulate the penis to become erect for the act of intercourse. Though this is not a function of the prostate, it is an important component that needs to be considered when prostate health is impeded and the prostate needs to be removed since the nerve runs along the side of the prostate. If the cancer lies close to this nerve, the nerve may be damaged when the prostate is removed, thus inhibiting normal erectile function.

Diseases of the Prostate

Only common diseases of the prostate will be discussed here, and those listed have similar symptoms to those expressed by cancer of the prostate. It stands to reason, then, that we look at the symptoms first.

You may experience some, but are unlikely to experience all, of the following symptoms, but remember, it doesn't mean that you have cancer of the prostate. The symptoms are:

- Increased frequency of urination, particularly at night

- Burning sensation or pain during urinating

- Slow start, with possible interruption of the flow of urine

- Blood in semen or urine

- Difficulty getting an erection

- Stiffness in lower back, hips, or upper thighs.

Enlargement of the prostate is common in men as they age and doesn't necessarily mean that cancer has, or will, develop. In fact, it has been said that every man, if he lives long enough, will suffer from an enlarged prostate at some time during his life. It has also been reported that the most common cause of prostate enlargement is due to benign prostatic hyperplasia (BPH).

Conditions that may affect the prostate and cause its enlargement include inflammation and infection.

The three main diseases of the prostate are:

- Prostatitis

- Benign prostatic hyperplasia (BPH)

- Cancer of the prostate

Prostatitis is the inflammation of the prostate due to bacterial or nonbacterial infection. The disease can be very painful and have a major affect on your quality of life. There are three main types of prostatitis that can affect men at any age. These are:

1. Acute *bacterial* prostatitis: This occurs when the prostate is infected by bacteria like *Escherichia coli* and *Klebsiella*. Inflammation of the prostate gland usually results from an infection that can cause severe complications if it is not treated promptly. It can be fatal if the bacterial infection is not treated and it travels in to the bloodstream (sepsis).

2. Chronic *bacterial* prostatitis: This results from the re-infection, or secondary infection of the prostate and urinary tract, resulting in inflammation. The symptoms are less severe than those associated with acute bacterial prostatitis.

3. Nonbacterial prostatitis: This is an inflamed prostate without bacterial infection. This is the least-known form of prostatitis since its cause is not understood. A form of nonbacterial prostatitis is chronic pelvic pain syndrome, which, as the name suggests, results in pain around the pelvic region.

Prostatitis is usually treated using antibiotics, but this may become less effective with re-infection, sometimes resulting in the need to have an operation called by the acronym TURPS (see below).

Benign prostatic hyperplasia (BPH) is the growth of the prostate due to noncancerous means. The prostate grows, doubling in size beyond puberty under the effects of testosterone. The growth rate slows down after about the age of twenty-five but may continue to grow later, resulting in BPH.

An effect of this growth is the restriction of urine flow by squeezing the urethra. If left untreated, it may cause problems for the bladder and possibly the kidneys. Again, the disease can be painful and seriously affect your quality of life.

BPH is an age-related disease with about one in seven men in their fifties suffering from it, and the figure increases with age. Day surgery is usually necessary to reduce the size of the prostate in severe cases by removing material around the urethra, thus reducing the pressure and restoring normal urine flow. This process is called a transurethral resection of the prostate (TURPS).

In less severe cases, watchful waiting, with a change in lifestyle (such as reducing caffeine intake) may suffice, while in other cases, alpha blockers (or alpha-adrenergic antagonists) can be used that relax the muscles in the prostate and urethra. Examples of alpha blockers include doxazosin and prazosin. The side effects of taking alpha blockers include low blood pressure, headache, and nausea, to name a few, but once again, your doctor will guide you should an alpha blocker be prescribed.

It is important to realise that prostatitis and BPH have no known links to cancer of the prostate, so it's in your interest to have a health check if you experience any of the symptoms listed above.

Cancer of the Prostate

This disease is often called the old man's disease since it mainly occurs in older men who are older than fifty. Because of our increase in life expectancy and other reasons unknown to us at this time, the incidence of prostate cancer has increased.

The cancer is aggressive if contracted by young men, but its growth rate slows the later it is contracted. For instance, if a man of seventy is diagnosed with prostate cancer, he is more likely to die of something else, rather than the cancer. He may die *with* the cancer but *not from* the cancer. My uncle is an example of someone dying with the disease but not as a result of the disease.

The development of cancer has been briefly defined and explained above. Here, though, it is described as the rapid growth of prostate cells, which lose their identity with other prostate cells and are, therefore, malignant. Other rapid growth types are noncancerous and are, therefore, benign— for example, BPH.

The earlier cancer of the prostate is diagnosed, the more likely it is that it can be eliminated. In the early stages, the cancer is likely to be found entirely within the prostate, hence the improved chance for its elimination and your survival.

If the cancer goes undetected, the chances for it to metastasize increase, as do the chances for this cancer to become more differentiated from prostate cells. Once the cells metastasize, the cells can migrate outside the prostate and spread to other regions in the body, thus decreasing the chances of the cancer being eliminated.

Prostate cancer outside of the prostate usually migrates to and affects the lymph nodes and bone marrow. That's why a lymph node is extracted during the operation to check whether the cancer has spread. A common site to which the cancer can spread is within the bones.

Like BPH, prostate cancer squeezes the urethra and therefore reduces urine flow, so the symptoms should be taken seriously.

The following diagram outlines the two possible scenarios for men over fifty who exhibit symptoms that result in swelling of the prostate.

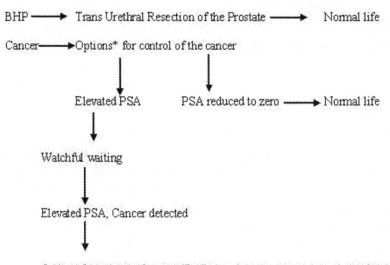

*The options for control of the cancer may be one or a combination of the following:

- ☐ Watchful waiting (particularly for men over seventy years)
- ☐ Prostatectomy (Keyhole, open abdomen)
- ☐ Radiation therapy
- ☐ Brachytherapy
- ☐ Hormone treatment
- ☐ Chemotherapy

Other options may also consist of procedures that have been introduced since writing this book or that were foreign to me.

Whichever options are presented to you, trust your doctor. Don't perform any self-diagnosis or listen to the anecdotes of others.

Final Words

Your experience with cancer of the prostate, or any other cancer, is unique. You may experience symptoms that are similar to those of another person, but your body may be reacting for entirely different reasons. Are you willing to take the risk? I'm certainly glad I didn't!

The only sure way to beat this disease is to take notice of the symptoms listed above and to trust your doctor. There are many treatments available for your consideration, and the sooner you react, the sooner you can get on with the rest of your life.

If you are over fifty, you should be having regular checkups. Don't let masculine pride get in the way. It has been said that men over fifty should be tested annually for cancer of the prostate. If you leave it any longer, then you might end up with the cancer in its *latter stages of growth.*

The reasons why we get cancer of the prostate are still uncertain, but the chances for a man to contract the disease are relatively high. About one in ten men will contract the disease, with the odds getting higher with age. So why take the chance! Take the plunge and have a regular checkup. *You are worth it, and so is your family.*

I have tried to be as honest as possible about the disease without using scare tactics. My experiences were real but not insurmountable. I won't say that I have developed any long-lasting emotional problems because of the disease. Once I believed that the cancer had been eliminated, I wanted to get on with my life, and this meant returning to normal thinking without any thought about the recurrence of the cancer.

Cancer of the prostate is not a death sentence *if you act promptly.* However, men do die from the disease because they fail to act. Prompt action is important.

Fear is one of the worst factors for this or any disease. If you don't get tested because you fear that you might be diagnosed with the disease, then chances are your inaction may result in a shortened life.

Why wait?

It is reasonably certain that you won't worry about the disease because you haven't been diagnosed with the disease. Nobody wants to think about the possibilities, but if you have any of the symptoms alluded to above, it is time to get tested. Overcome the fear of the test and visit your doctor.

Finally, don't hide the fact that you have cancer of the prostate, should you be diagnosed with the disease. Your family needs to know that you are happy with your life. I asked my wife if she thought about the cancer and whether she believed that it might return. Happily, she didn't. She had the same attitude as I had; the cancer has gone.

Imagine if your partner held the belief that the cancer might return and you didn't know this. What agony would that person be going through unnecessarily? Talk about it. Dispel any fears, and get on with life. As I have said repeatedly throughout the book, you are worth it.

I would like to point to the fact that cancer doesn't discriminate. You know this, but it is worth noting since many well-known entities have succumbed to cancer, like Ted Whitten, a famous and much-loved Australian rules football player. I remember seeing Ted being honoured by an adoring crowd of footy enthusiasts days before he died. Michael Corby, father of Schapelle Corby, a convicted drug runner, died of cancer of the prostate that had spread to his bones. Michael fought to get his daughter released from an Indonesian prison. And more recently, Jane McGrath, wife of an Australian test cricketer Glenn McGrath set up the McGrath Foundation to fight breast cancer, the disease to which she succumbed after a long battle.

None of these people wanted to die. Each had something to live for. They fought it in their own way, but the cancer had a strong hold.

Advice Summary

Throughout this book, I have been giving advice to the reader should he suspect that he is having problems with his prostate. If you suspect that you may be having problems with your prostate:

- ☐ Visit your doctor and have the appropriate health test. Don't wait.

- ☐ Discuss the condition with your partner.

- ☐ Stay positive. Doom and gloom gets you nowhere.

- ☐ Exercise, even if you walk five to six km (two to three miles).

- ☐ Eat healthily; junk food can't possibly be helping.

- ☐ Learn a relaxation technique, such as yoga, tai chi, or meditation.

- ☐ Visualize success. A negative image may promote the disease.

- ☐ Take prescribed medication as directed. Don't self-medicate or remove yourself from your doctor's prescribed medicines.

- ☐ Talk about the disease; don't hide it. You may help others.

- ☐ Take advice from your doctor, not well-meaning friends.

Depression

Introduction

By using the term depression here, I don't mean a bump in the road or a hollowed-out section of ground. Depression is a mental disorder that many people *avoid* talking about. In fact, many will deny the suggestion that they may be depressed; such is the stigma behind this simple word.

I am not a doctor of medicine, nor am I a doctor of psychology. I am a person who has suffered from depression at all levels, and believe me, it is not a condition I would wish upon anybody. This section is based upon my experience with depression, including my most recent bout of a major depressive episode where I fell into the pits of hell.

I use simple language so a novice can understand the terminology, thus giving him or her, or you, an understanding of this insidious disease. The most important outcome I could wish for you by reading this book is that you take the appropriate steps towards alleviating the disease by going to see your doctor or encouraging a loved one you suspect is suffering from depression to see a doctor. Don't let your self-talk talk you out of seeing a health specialist.

I also hope that by reading this book you will identify issues for yourself with regards to depression. It is not a book about treating depression; the treatment is determined by your attending health authorities. However, by reading the material in this book, you should be able to conclude that help is certainly available and you should see for yourself that you are not the only person suffering from depression. Depression can be treated.

Men are a funny lot. Bravado is not a solution but a roadblock, yet many men employ it the moment there is a hint of trouble with their health. My depression developed after an operation for cancer of the prostate. It wasn't automatic *but developed over a period of time.* Hey! I wasn't thinking of the cancer; I believed and still believe that it has gone. The depression came out of nowhere, possibly a side effect of medication or the trauma of the operation. Besides, I will admit that I am not normally a positive person and had to learn to be positive, and that was with a struggle.

It is also important to note that people experiencing a chronic illness *may* experience depression, since depression has been linked to chronic illness. This *does not* mean that an individual will become depressed.

My Treatment Disclosure

Nobody likes to think that he or she suffers from depression. The very word has connotations of not coping, and let's face it, we all like to believe that we are coping with life. Hell, I didn't want to believe that I was depressed!

I went to see my doctor, who diagnosed me with depression. *Shit!* I thought. *What now?*

He prescribed the antidepressant Zoloft, which I took religiously for two years, but it didn't *seem* to be working, so he changed the prescription to another antidepressant, Effexor. Two years on this drug saw no *apparent* change either, so he suggested that I see a psychiatrist.

The psychiatrist was a great guy, but I still suffered from depression. He prescribed Cymbalta, which also didn't work—or *so I thought.* There wasn't much counselling between us, just questions about my feelings and modification to the amount of antidepressant I should take.

I didn't see any point in taking antidepressants; none of them seemed to work, so I, with my limited knowledge of the drug, told the psychiatrist that I wanted to come off the antidepressant since there didn't seem to be any change in my feelings. I stopped taking the drug. I came off it by small decreases in the dosage, and at last, I was drug free. Did I feel any different? I didn't think so, until an incident occurred where "I spat the dummy" and went into a rage of temper.

At this stage, I had been free of antidepressants for about one month. It was after my period of dabbling in alternative medicines; more on that later. *Hell! What was that about? Maybe I need to be on antidepressants after all,* I thought. But not me. I didn't want to be on drugs. The bloody things don't work—*do they?*

Two weeks later, I had another hissy fit. This time I spiralled into the pits of hell and couldn't get out, not without support. I was drug free and suffering a major depression, so guess what? The antidepressants were working after all, and I went back on Cymbalta.

The point to this story is, you might think that the antidepressant isn't working because you feel no different, but maybe we become acclimatized to the drug and believe we feel no different since, after all, the antidepressant should take the depression away, shouldn't it? At least that was my view of the medication.

Also, don't take yourself off the medication without your doctor's assistance and without proper monitoring. I told my doctor but kept everything to myself. Who wants to talk about depression? It's a dreary subject.

My Major Depression Moment

As I have alluded to above, *I suffer from depression.* I thought I knew all about it until I hit the wall over a simple altercation. Isn't it silly? I can't remember what triggered the episode, but it came on with a vengeance.

I became moody and instantly set about not talking to anyone. I went to my bedroom and lay on the bed, falling deeper into depression. Self-loathing was the order of the moment. I hated myself. Who would want to talk to me? Why did my wife stay with a loser like me? The more I thought about it, the deeper I fell.

How did I feel? It is difficult to describe. I never felt so lousy in all my life. In fact, life wasn't worth considering. Why should I think about others? They don't care about me. I wasn't worth considering. In fact, I couldn't even say I; it was too personal. Everybody left me alone for a short time, and as far as I was concerned, good. Let me be; I needed no one.

Did I eat dinner that night? No way! I had secretly decided to end it all by not eating or drinking, and for two days, I didn't touch any food or liquid. Nobody was going to get me to eat; I wanted to die, and this was my way of doing it.

Once my wife understood what I was doing, she rallied the family. My sons and daughters came over to stay with us while I continued to wallow in self-pity. My youngest son tried to talk me out of my state and tried to encourage me to eat, but no way. I wanted to die. *Stuff you all,* I thought.

My daughters told me that they loved me and that I was still needed, but ha! It was a trick to get me to eat. I wasn't going to fall for that old line. I had to be greedy if I was to achieve my goal. I loved my family, but they'd get over it—my death, I mean.

No amount of talk helped. I was in control, and life wasn't worth living. I continued to fall into the pit of despair. I sighed a lot, hid my face from everyone, and told everyone to leave me alone. "You don't have a right to do this, Dad. We all need you." *To hell with you all,* was my way of thinking.

Towards evening on the first day, I thought, *Hell, she's getting help. I've got to get out of here,* so I picked up my keys and ran to my car, followed by a distressed wife. I drove to a place where no one would find me. *Bastards. Who do they think they are?* I thought. I told them to leave me. *I'll sit here until I die. Stuff you all.* So I sat in my car, off the road in an isolated place, and thought about what had just transpired. I was free of any interference, alone with my thoughts. *No, they shouldn't suffer. It's me I don't like,* I thought, so I drove home again and walked into a house filled with concerned relatives.

When I walked inside, I insulted my brother-in-law, who was concerned for my wellbeing, and I returned to my bedroom to continue my sulking.

My brother-in-law tried to pacify me, but to no avail. "Piss off," I told him.

The next day, my eldest son flew in from interstate and told me he wasn't going home until I came to my senses. I laughed and said, "It should take about four days, so you can stay if you want." He left me to wallow in my negative thoughts. Little did I know that he, my daughters, and my wife had started to get help from outside. Did I care? No way!

Later in the morning, my son and wife came into the room to talk to me. I sulked. My wife touched my hand and said, "Come on, love, let us help you." That was all it took! I broke down and cried like a baby—worse, in fact, since I hid myself under the blankets and kicked like a spoilt brat. I could feel my wife and son stroking my back through the blankets, but I could only cry. "Leave me alone," I said through my tears and heavy feeling of despair. They left me alone.

After I had finished crying, I sat up. *Shit! What am I doing?* I thought. *Why the hell do I want to kill myself? Why am I listening to my self-talk? I can beat this? This is ridiculous*, I said to myself while wiping my tears. Since I was sitting, I decided to put on my slippers and go to the kitchen to eat. My resolve was weakening.

Need I say that my family were elated and offered me a seat while someone got me a cup of tea. I started to say, "I want to stop" but couldn't. I broke down once more and cried, hiding my face behind my hands in shame. What an idiot I was!

I sat and regained my composure when the phone rang. It was a member of the mental health crisis team. "Dad, will you speak to this woman from mental health? She will help you over all this," my son asked.

"Sure," I said as I took the phone. But when I tried to speak to the counsellor, I broke down again and blubbered. My son took the phone and spoke to her, but moments later, I regained my composure and spoke into the phone. Support is out there, believe me.

From that moment on, I took control over my life and decided to join the rest of the world and live my life fully. I needed support and went to see the psychiatrist and a crisis counsellor who was a trained psychologist.

I hope my account shocked you. Don't feel pity for me; depression is a disorder that needs support, not pity. I entered the state of severe depression because of my *negative* self-talk and I believe, because I had taken myself off the medication. It was my fault that I ended up where I dared to go, and you know what? *I didn't care,* and this is the factor that can *end* a life. I was lucky that I didn't choose a method that was quicker, like overdosing or slashing my wrist. Deep down, I could have been crying for help; I don't know.

You know what! I think we learn which tools to use when we suffer despair. Unfortunately, I experienced a second fall into deep depression, but this time, I simply sat and moped around. I didn't speak, and believe me, this is one of my major faults when I suffer so deeply. I clam up and say nothing, so how can I expect support? Second, and more importantly, my reasoning changed. Now I was saying to myself, *If anyone gives you the shits, take all of your pills. That'll stuff them up. It'll be too late.*

How stupid! How utterly ridiculous, but this is the thinking when you suffer deep depression. I had actually reasoned a more definite method of ending it all. *Please, talk to your partner,* anyone, and *do not listen to your own self-talk.* I have been to hell and back twice, and life is worth considering—with me in the picture. Isn't this what I wanted after the cancer operation? And what, depression was going to change all that? Talk, don't hide it.

A Definition

Before I go any further with the discussion on depression, I want to give you a definition of the term. The definition is not mine but has been repeated in many psychology textbooks and is relevant here.

Depression: a mood disorder where people show *extreme* and *persistent* sadness, despair, and loss of interest in life's general activities.

Notice the emphasis on the words extreme and persistent. We all get depressed from time to time. The death of a loved one, for instance, can leave an individual depressed, but under normal circumstances, we get over it. Yes, we grieve and feel miserable and may even cry, but with the passage of time, we get over the death and life goes on. What is important in the definition of depression is that the effect (sadness, despair, sleeplessness, loss of interest, and so on*) is long lasting and extreme.* Exhibiting the feeling of despair does not mean that you are a long-term depressive. Feelings of despair that have occurred over a long period of time and that persist may *suggest* that you suffer from depression. It is important that you understand this.

What is *not* normal about life is when the depressive feeling becomes pervasive, *and doesn't go away.* Remember, depression is a disorder, not the norm. Many people live without feeling depressed, so why should you suffer from it if something can be done about alleviating the problem?

Note too that unlike other diseases, depression exhibits only psychological characteristics such as tardy behaviour, negative thoughts, and poor feelings. There are no lesions, no failing organs, or no other physical sign that you are suffering from depression, yet it originates within the brain through an imbalance of certain neurotransmitters. The definition defines depression through what can be expressed psychologically; the chemical imbalance, a physical cause, is what is being addressed when you take antidepressants.

Symptoms of Depression

When depression is pervasive (long lasting), it is known as a major depressive disorder and can have one or more of the following symptoms.

- Loss of interest in life's activities
- Sadness
- Feeling of hopelessness
- Negative mood
- Loss of sleep
- Loss of appetite
- Lethargy
- Loss of self-esteem

- Guilt

- Feeling unworthy

- Indecisiveness

I would like to add to the list by stating that depressed individuals procrastinate more than others and sigh a lot more. Also, depressed individuals are more pessimistic than others, though it would be wrong to say that pessimists suffer from depression.

Please understand that you do not need to have all of the characteristics identified above, only some, and they must be ongoing. If ever you have any doubt about it, speak to your doctor or read articles on depression. Visit sites on the Internet about depression. "Beyond Blue" www.**beyondblue**.org.au/ is one great site, and it offers some very helpful information. Think about how often and for how long you have experienced one or more of the above characteristics. Did they go away quickly? Do they still exist? What are you going to do about it?

If the symptoms persist and maybe grow, it is highly probable *that suicide* may be contemplated. Once you start to think about suicide, it is very likely you are having a major depressive episode. *You will need to do something about it straight away.* Talk to someone, anyone, and then see your doctor. Do not let the moment work itself into your psyche; it isn't worth it. Call a help line. *Talk, but **not** to yourself.*

Let's look at each symptom for depression in turn.

1. Loss of interest in life's activities.

It is reasonable to assume that life is meant to be lived without considering whether you should be part of it. I mean, when we get up in the morning, we don't think, *Should I be part of life today?* It sounds silly, doesn't it?

At times, though, we experience psychological ups and downs, and it is when the downs become overwhelming, or we believe that they are overwhelming, that we may think about our place in this big universe. You could be led to think negatively about an activity that should and could be done, *Stuff it, I won't bother. It doesn't matter anyway,* so you lose interest in a little bit of your life. If you experience more failure, you could lose more interest in life, leading you to believe that life would be better without you.

Life is challenging. It has its ups and downs, and these moments are not meant to be personal. Think about the good times in your life. Don't they outweigh the poor times? Why let one poor moment destroy your life? We all live on the same planet and all suffer from time to time with failure and/or loss of interest. Some people get over it quickly. Those who suffer depression are *no worse* than those who regain quick control, so why should they or you think about ending it all? It's the depression talking, not the person. Don't let the depression define who you are.

Isn't the belief that "life would be better without me" an irrational belief? Of course it is, so challenge the belief. Seek support from a counsellor.

2. Sadness

We all get sad from time to time. The loss of a loved one, or even when your footy team loses, can make one feel sad. There is nothing wrong with this. However, when the sadness persists, that is when you need to seek help. Normal sadness if such a thing exists is normally short lived. We get over it, and life goes on.

If you are feeling sad for no apparent reason, take a look at your environment. Do you work in a dark, unlit place? Is it winter and you have been inside most of the time? You may be suffering from seasonal adjusted depression (SAD) and need more sun light.

Sadness is a normal emotion and we have the right to experience it. But when it persists, that is when you should seek help. When your football team loses the finals, you get over it, and so it should be with other life activities.

3. Feeling of hopelessness

Did you have any subjects at school where you performed poorly? Did you think, *I'm hopeless at this subject*? If so, feeling hopeless is quite normal. We all feel uncomfortable in certain situations, even hopeless at performing a task, but when we take this hopelessness into our everyday life and feel its pain often, that is when hopelessness will lead towards depression.

It is not normal to feel forever hopeless. Remember, when the symptoms are pervasive, you need to do something about it. Once you get into your mindset or make a habit of feeling hopeless, you will dig yourself deeper into the hopelessness well and find it difficult to climb out. Learnt hopelessness is like this. Yes, we do learn to be hopeless, and it isn't pretty.

You are not hopeless. More often than not, practice is all you need to perform a task well. Even in a relationship, put in the extra effort to make it work; don't give up. The feeling will go away if you contribute positively to alleviating the situation that created the feeling. At no time is anyone meant to forever feel hopeless. Remember the old saying, "If it is to be, *it is up to me.*"

4. Negative mood

Again, we all occasionally suffer from a negative mood state. The car breaks down and you can't go to the football. You are bound to feel poorly about it, don't you think? The mood state might last the whole day, but you do get over it. If in two weeks' time you are still dwelling on not going to the footy, then something is wrong. Many things will go wrong in life. Some will cause us to feel poorly about it for a while, while others won't make a dent in life at all.

Negative moods will come and go. But guess what! If the negative mood stays, then it is time to get help. You don't need to suffer. It's not a woe is me moment; it is depression. Seek help.

5. Loss of sleep

I will admit that I am a poor sleeper. I think about things for far too long before going to sleep, and consequently, I often do not get to sleep until very late. My wife can drop off to sleep within five minutes of going to bed.

If I am developing an idea for a book or a class lesson, I seem to feel all right the next morning despite the poor sleep I endured. However, if I am dwelling on something that happened during the day and my thoughts are negative, the next morning, I continue to feel poorly, even though I might not be thinking about the previous day's activity.

In bed, you are on your own. Your thoughts can turn sour, and you can dwell on them because *you own them*. You have all the time in the world to think about the event that has upset you, and in this hazy moment of sleeplessness, you can very easily rationalize that you were treated harshly. *It's not fair. Life shouldn't deal such harsh blows*; or so your thinking goes.

When we lose sleep, particularly over long periods of time, our thinking can get disturbed and irrational. If this persists, then the thinking may become increasingly more negative. So, if you lack sleep for extended periods of time, speak to your doctor. Seek help.

6. Loss of appetite

There may be times when we don't feel like eating, particularly at the onset of a cold or flu or any other illness. During times of mourning, we can often feel like not eating, and when we are feeling low, a loss of appetite can be experienced.

But it is these negative feelings that can lead towards depression, and consequently, if you are feeling low for an extended period of time, you may also experience a loss of appetite for this same period. When you don't eat or drink, you *feed* the depression and fall deeper into the pit of despair. I know, I have been there. I stopped eating and drinking, and during this time, I didn't feel that I needed food. I didn't feel hungry. *Nothing except my change in thinking caused me to eat.*

If you have lost your appetite, take a look at your life to see what could be causing it and question your beliefs. Again, if you can't make improvements, seek help.

7. Lethargy

Sometimes it's just hard to make a start, particularly if you lack confidence in finishing what you need to do. You drag your feet, complain about doing the job, and feel miserable, but you get the job done and the weight is lifted.

Kids are great lethargic strategists. "Ah, do I have to? I'm tired. Can I do it tomorrow? I don't feel too good." You've heard it and have probably said it yourself. But again, if you feel this way every time you have to perform a task, then it is time to do something about it. Lethargy is not a normal, everyday function. Yes, we can feel lethargic from time to time, but we are supposed to get over it. Lethargy is a great precursor for procrastination. Imagine feeling lethargic every day. Hey! Why not leave it till tomorrow? You will feel better; until the task needs to be done, and then you feel poorly again. Ah, it's a vicious cycle.

8.   Loss of self-esteem

Low self esteem—the confidence breaker and soul destroyer. Think about it. If you feel that you can't do anything right, how confident will you be with life? I've got to say, though, that the term self-esteem is very general. An individual can lack self-esteem in performing a particular task yet be high in esteem elsewhere. At school, for instance, a student can have low esteem with regards to mathematics but be high in esteem everywhere else.

Self-esteem is related to self-concept, and our concept of self is built from the sum of our experiences and thoughts. If the sum of our experiences is negative for a particular task, then we can expect to have low esteem about our ability to perform well with the continuation of that task. But it shouldn't be about the way we think about the task. Yes, I might be poor in maths, but if I change my study habits and the way I think about maths, I can improve.

Life throws curveballs at us from time to time. It is when we believe, "I can't do anything," that we lack general self-esteem. But nobody is so bad that he or she should paint him or herself in a bad light. Hell, we all have bad times, and sometimes they are protracted. It isn't aimed at me or you; it happens, and we are unprepared for it. Build confidence, have a go, ask for help, do it with someone else, but never say, "I am hopeless. I can't do this."

9.   Feeling guilty

When we tell a lie, we can sometimes feel guilty. This is normal. Doing something behind someone's back can also lead to guilty feelings. Again, this is normal. There are probably hundreds of situations that can lead an individual to feel guilty, all normal. However, just like everything else I have said above, it is when the feelings of guilt are protracted or occur very often that is not normal and should be addressed. Guilt can lead to high anxiety, which in turn may lead to depression if the reasons behind the guilt are not addressed.

10. Feeling unworthy

I fell into this category and spiralled into a deep depression. I felt that I was unworthy of the love of others. "Why would anyone love me? I don't deserve it." Yep, been there, and it wasn't good. There are other reasons for feeling unworthy; maybe for a promotion, praise for a job you performed, or simply for birthday good wishes. I suspect that unworthiness fits in with disliking oneself. If you are not happy with yourself, why would you feel worthy of anything?

Yet, why not! Hell, if you've done something that others believe to be great or you yourself would have thought great if someone else did it, then why shouldn't you receive praise? Why wouldn't you be worthy? Low self-worth, like low self-esteem, can be soul destroying, yet there is no valid reason for either in your life. You and I are no different from anyone else on this planet, so why should I think that I am unworthy? Why is another person more worthy than me? If they get higher grades or performed better at a task, then yes, they may be worthy of more praise, but if I do just as good as anyone else at a task, then I am no less worthy than anyone else.

Take another look at the list above. Every one of the symptoms is psychological. Every one stems from the way we think, particularly about ourselves. I used to think that life was crap and that I was a pathetic person, but not anymore and you know what? Suddenly life is fantastic and I want to live it fully with my wife and family.

Think about yourself. If you believe that some of these symptoms or characteristics apply to you, then seek help. At the very least, believe that you are worth saving and life will go on, so be part of life. You're worth every effort. Get out of the rut that may lead to a more sinister ending to your depression. Believe me, you do not want to go there.

How Do Others View Depression?

I have already admitted that I suffer from depression while others in my family don't. How do they view the disorder? Do they expect that all you need to do is get your act together?

I get advice from time to time from people who obviously do not suffer from the malady. "Come on, pull yourself together," I have heard. Even, "Get over it" has been used to encourage me to join the normal people in society. A deep sigh and miserable look on one's face does not mean that a happy slap on the back from a well-meaning friend will snap one out of one's depressed mood.

Read the history of depression below and you'll see that forever, people have not fully understood what depression is. Families used to incarcerate their loved ones if they suffered from the disorder.

I understand that if you have never suffered depression, or have been on the receiving end, then you do not understand what is required of the depressed individual to snap out of it. For sure, the effects upon you of someone else's mood state can be debilitating, but a quick cure does not exist. It takes time to get oneself out of a depressed state. Remember, when an individual is depressed, his or her thinking will be such that the depressed mood state will be *maintained*, not dissipated. *If I am unworthy, then wallowing in self-pity is my right. I deserve it.*

History of Depression

I will be very general here; people and dates will be overlooked. What is important is how we have changed with regards to the treatment and understanding of depression.

Let's go back to about 450 BC. Way back then, there were no doctors, just people who knew things. They were *learned people,* our early scientists, I suppose. It used to be believed that everything consisted of four elements, earth, fire, water, and air, and these elements were also related to various parts of our body. Consider the list below. The elements are matched with the relevant humour located in a specific organ.

- Earth   Phlegm (in the brain)

- Fire   Blood (the heart)

- Water   Yellow bile (the liver)

- Air   Black bile (the spleen)

It was believed that when an affected individual breathed air, he also breathed black bile, which would go to the brain to cause the exhibited phenomena or mental illness. The word melancholy means *black bile,* and its specific effects exhibit the same effects as what we call depression today.

Way back then, all mental illnesses were put into one basket, so to speak. In fact, as time progressed, people were institutionalized because of their mental disorders. Mental illnesses were often thought to be the work of the devil, so such activities as bloodletting were used to release the bad spirits.

Who were the blood letters? Why, the local barber since he had the apparatus for cutting, even if it was for hair. Imagine going to the local barber. "What's it going to be today, hair cut or bloodletting?" "Oh, bloodletting, thanks, only don't cut too deep into the jugular."

Sometimes, a crack would be made in the individual's skull to let the evil spirits out. Of course, the usual outcome for bloodletting and cracking the skull was death, but at least the individual died with clean spirits.

Around 100 BC, there were two schools of thought explaining depression, the physical school (explained above) and the emotional school, which of course is closer to the truth. Neglect of reason was one way of explaining mental illness, and a little later predetermined personalities, since people who were by nature angry or sad suffered from melancholia.

With the advancement of time, nervous disorders became related to melancholia since they were basically due to a person's disposition, whereas other mental diseases still belonged to the devil and bad spirits.

During the early period of Christianity, the priests of the time had a strong hold on the beliefs and well being of their congregations, and since the people needed something to believe in, mental disorders were again attributed to *bad spirits*. Fear was often used to control the populous, and before long, witches were burnt at the stake, along with anyone else who might have exhibited a behaviour *not commensurate* with the general public.

But time has its way of changing our beliefs. Mental institutions became abundant and were dumping grounds for the mentally ill, where the inmates were shown as *curiosities* to the general public.

In the 1700s, depression used to be known as the death syndrome since many seriously depressed individuals used to *report* that they would be *better off dead*. Some actually achieved death through suicide. Because the mentally ill used to be institutionalized, it was seen as a stigma within a family, who would never admit to anyone that someone in the family suffered from the malady. Ah, ignorance. It's bliss; or is it!

Melancholia, the older name for depression, was probably seen as a mild form of mental illness, or at the very least, a person who was melancholy may not have exhibited some of the extreme factors, such as violence or rambling, which could have resulted institutionalization. Feelings of melancholia include feeling down, lethargic, not wanting to talk, and possibly self-loathing, so people who were melancholy *probably kept to themselves and escaped persecution.*

Happily, though, people who were institutionalized during the eighteenth century were looked after by their carers since this was a time of great humanity, and mentally ill people were meant to be treated in a humanitarian way. There were other changes in beliefs about mental illness, such as conflict with one's conscience, but it is sufficient to stop here and contemplate our future. I only wanted to demonstrate that how we have changed our thinking about depression has led to greater good and why it is more accepted in the general community.

When I say that the mentally ill were looked after by their carers, it wasn't without its fair share of cruelty. Patients were often locked up in a confined space if they didn't do what they were told or given some crude form of shock treatment, which demonstrated the patients' illness through the electric current causing contortions in the face. "Of course he is mad. Look at his face."

In 1872, in Melbourne, Australia, the Kew cottages were built for the mentally ill. Most patients died within the institution, shunned by their family, and many patients suffered from such accepted disorders as depression and dementia. Such was the ignorance of early psychiatry. Yet, strangely enough, this same ignorance has led to the knowledge we have today where people are no longer institutionalized.

It's possible that our attitude about depression stemmed from beliefs of old, or at least the stigma is still felt, so instead of talking about our feelings, we keep the fact that we may be depressed to ourselves.

Depression Statistics

Depression in the Western world is becoming a problem and is predicted to become one of the biggest killers within our society. Consider the following statistics:

- One in five people will experience depression in their lifetime, and *over 50 percent of the depressed do not seek treatment.*

- This year alone (2010) one million people in Australia will experience a depressive illness.

- Depression is the *third largest* individual health problem in Australia after heart disease and stroke.

- In the workplace, depression accounts for six million working days lost each year.

- About 20 percent of people will be affected by depression, and 6 percent will experience a major depressive illness.

Postnatal depression affects between 10 to 20 percent of all new mothers to some degree.

- The rate of increase of depression among children is 23 percent p.a. and is increasing amongst *preschoolers.*

- 15 percent of the population of most developed countries suffers severe depression.

- 30 percent of women are depressed. Men's figures were previously thought to be half that of women, but new estimates are higher.

- 54 percent of people believe depression is a personal weakness.

- 41 percent of depressed women are too embarrassed to seek help.

- 80 percent of depressed people are *not* currently having any treatment.

- 92 percent of depressed African American males do not seek treatment.

- 15 percent of depressed people will *commit suicide.*

- Depression will be the second largest killer after heart disease by 2020—and studies show depression is a contributory factor to fatal coronary disease.

- Depression results in more absenteeism than almost any other physical disorder

(Various Sources, 2010)

Please note, when you read statistics, they are not saying that you will get or that you have a high likelihood of becoming depressed. The figures will vary slightly from year to year and from country to country, though generally, the changes will be small. The statistics are evidence that depression is prevalent within our society and only reports recorded incidences. How many people suffer depression in silence?

Consider too the incidence of depression in children, an increase of 23 percent per year. Depression is also increasing amongst preschoolers. How on earth do preschoolers suffer depression? Yet the statistics say they do. Not a pretty picture for the future, is it? Notice too the high percentage of people who do not seek help. *They suffer in silence.* Why?

Depression Is Not a Crime

I have already alluded to the fact that I get depressed. I get seriously depressed. In fact, I get seriously pissed off by many things when I am depressed; *I hate the feeling. But I can talk about it.* Depression is not a crime. I talk about it to my friends, and they are still my friends. Even my students knew that I suffered depression.

I once asked a group of students if any of them suffered from depression, and in a class of twenty-six, three said yes. One was being treated for the disorder. Now, I didn't ask the group to tell me there and then yes. I asked publically but said that they could report to me privately and only if they wanted, since, like adults, kids don't want their peers to know that they get depressed.

I measured depression in a school of year nine students when I was studying for my PhD. Again, I found that there were kids who were considered, according to the results in the questionnaire, to be seriously depressed. Two of them were later verified to be clinically depressed. The students didn't die, nor did they leave the school. They were treated for depression and continued to study, *without the other students knowing* that they had been identified as being depressed. So, *depression is not isolated to an age level.*

Nobody is immune to depression. Yes, normally our youth are not subject to depression at a high rate. What I have stated above might seem like an epidemic, but the truth is, depression is normally a disorder for older people, though evidence exists that depression in our young is on the increase.

I once suffered serious depression where I felt like speaking to nobody. I was driving to work and remember thinking, *If I had an accident now, it would be all over. Nobody would miss me. Besides, they'd get over it.* I didn't listen to music or any radio, for that matter, while driving. I felt absolutely miserable, to use an absolute term. Did I talk myself out of it? No way! I was depressed, and **my thinking** kept it that way and you know what? To me, **that was how it should have been.** There was no relief because I believed that what I was going through at that moment was good and proper. That's it! I should be depressed.

Nobody could help me. I was wallowing in a sea of self-pity. Isn't it pathetic?

Well, no, I don't believe that it was pathetic since *I wasn't in control.* I was too deep into a depressed state to bother about doing anything to change the state, but I'm out of it now. How? I worked as hard as I could at my job to forget about my mood, and when I had *come down* a little, I then worked on my mood state and thinking.

Depression is not a great feeling, and we don't have to suffer if we are willing to work at reducing its effects.

Depression in the Family

If a family member has depression, there is a higher likelihood of depression continuing within the family. The study of twins verifies this statement. Identical twins are both more likely to have depression, even if they are *separated at birth, if depression is in the family.* Note that the *likelihood* is more likely, not definitely. Non-identical twin studies have shown that it is not equally likely that the twins will develop depression if it was in the family. So seeing a loved one in the family suffer from depression *does not mean* that you will also suffer. The hereditary factor was recognized in the very early period of human development and was hinted at above when I mentioned predetermined personalities. Such personalities were often seen within the family of the person affected.

Depression can be treated psychologically. Depending on the psychologist's training, you may be told that it is the way you think—dwelling on negative thoughts. You may be told that it's in the words you use, such as *must* and *should*. Both words are absolute, and depending on how they are used, they may lead to negative consequences. However you are treated, you can be sure that the method used will be successful *if you participate fully.* More on this later.

Depression can be treated chemically (described below), but no matter how the depression is treated, the depression process is carried out in our brain. The treatment might be psychological, but depending on how you view the treatment, whether you take the treatment seriously will govern how your brain will react to the treatment.

Why is this important? Because when one is depressed, the individual is less likely to react positively unless he or she trusts the counsellor or participates fully in the program offered. *Paying lip service to anything generally results in failure.*

To say that depression is a mood disorder where people show *extreme* and *persistent* sadness, despair, and loss of interest in life's general activities is to say nothing at all about the mechanism of depression. To list the symptoms is to say nothing about the mechanism. Yes, to know the symptoms is important in identifying the problem, but what is this thing called depression—how does it act? To answer this question, we need to have a look at the brain, or at least part of the brain.

The Depression Mechanism

Let me say from the outset that I am not an expert on brain theory. It has been said that depression is not a single disorder but a symptom of many conditions. In this section, I am only attempting to explain the mechanism of depression in layman's terms. There may be other factors that I have not described, but what is important here is the fact that a simple mechanism is provided for you so you can see how it acts within your body. The *treatment* is between you and your doctor.

The brain of a depressed person is less active during depression than the brain of a normal person. Depressed people are less inclined to take action and to reason rationally than non-depressed people. I hope that my description will help you to understand this.

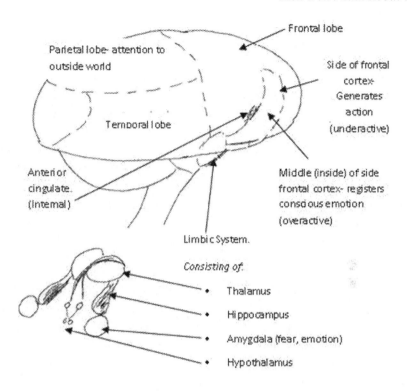

Parietal lobe- attention to
outside world

Frontal lobe

Side of frontal
cortex-
Generates
action
(underactive)

Temporal lobe

Anterior
cingulate.
(Internal)

Middle (inside) of side
frontal cortex- registers
conscious emotion
(overactive)

Limbic System.

Consisting of:

* Thalamus
* Hippocampus
* Amygdala (fear, emotion)
* Hypothalamus

Right side of brain and limbic system

Consider the diagram of the right side of the brain. In depressed people, the side frontal cortex that helps generate *action* is *underactive*, and the middle of the side frontal cortex that registers conscious *emotion* is *overactive*. Together, they result in an individual who is loath to take action and is likely to feel miserable about taking the action. If you have suffered from depression, you know what I mean. In fact, the decision to take no action supports my conjecture that depressed people are more likely to procrastinate, or be more indecisive, than non-depressed people. Take me as an example; I am a chronic procrastinator, and I have a PhD on the subject to prove it!

The limbic system is largely responsible for the activities described above. More information flows out of the limbic system than inwards. So with depressed people, the reduced response to the limbic system results in depression, resulting in inaction, poor memory, reduced thinking ability, and the feelings associated with depression. It is the *limbic system* that is largely responsible for *fear* and the *stress reaction*, and when the system is not functioning freely, it can lead to *depression*.

The limbic system consists of a number of components; the *hippocampus* has *memory* of *sad/happy* events, whereas the *amygdala* is responsible for generating *feelings*. It has been said that in depressed individuals, the hippocampus may reduce in size and the amygdala grow. So, if the part responsible for memory of feelings, and which makes decisions about the feelings, is impaired, then whatever the amygdala presents will be experienced. The amygdala will feed negative feelings to the conscious mind, inhibiting action. If a region in the frontal lobe draws on the memories of such feelings, the result won't be happiness, and the cingulate cortex will fasten on those negative feelings. Ah, the woes of the depressed!

The biological explanation of depression is more complex than a psychological description, but I think it is important for you to understand that what the doctor or psychologist is trying to do to alleviate the problem of depression affects what happens in your brain. It is more complex than what I have provided, but so you can understand how antidepressants work, I now need to go into a little more detail about how neurological messages are transmitted, particularly around the limbic system and regions associated with the limbic system.

I plan to generalize, so please, don't give up on the description offered.

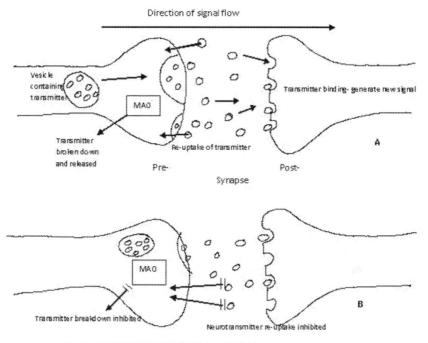

Neuron action A: normal, B: Antidepressant action

Consider the diagram of two neurons (nerve cells) above. There are millions of neurons in the brain that are intricately connected to other neurons through a network. Each neuron is not physically connected to other neurons, and there is a gap between connecting neurons. Neurotransmitter chemicals cross the gap, thus firing the second neuron or if you like, saying, "Here is the signal. Keep it going." This is the synapse. In the absence of neurotransmitters, no signal is transmitted. That part is easy, but what happens if there is a reduction in the amount of neurotransmitters? Yes, you've guessed it; depression can result, depending on where it occurs.

The neurotransmitters reported here are the monoamines serotonin and norepinephrine. A reduction in each of these is seen in depressed people compared to non-depressed individuals. Dopamine is another transmitter but in abundance, it produces mania. There are other transmitting chemicals, but for simplicity, it is sufficient to use the two named for the explanation.

The presynaptic neuron makes the neurotransmitter serotonin or norepinephrine (diagram A above), which are *encapsulated* in a vesicle. The vesicle *migrates* towards the transmission end of the neuron where the serotonin and norepinephrine are *released*. Once released, the *transmitter crosses* the synaptic gap and *binds* with the receiver end of the *receiving* neuron. This triggers *the manufacture* and release of the transmitter at the transmission end of the neuron, and the process is *repeated* until it reaches the desired target.

What is important here is the fact that this takes place within the region of the limbic system that is responsible for feelings and emotions. The quality of the signal is degraded for depressed people. Note that the transmitter passes across the gap and some of it is *absorbed back* into the presynaptic neuron (re-uptake), where mono-amine oxidase (MAO) breaks it down.

In depressed individuals, the amount of neurotransmitter is *reduced*. This could be due to higher *re-uptake*, more *active MAO*, and/or insufficient receiver sites on the receiving neuron. Whatever the cause, reduction in the amount of transmitter leads to depression.

To increase the amount of transmitter, antidepressants can be used (this is the chemical treatment for depression). There are two main types, those that *block re-uptake* and those *that inhibit the action of MAO* (diagram B above). In either case, the net result is an increase in the amount of serotonin or norepinephrine.

There are many brands and types of antidepressants, so speak to your doctor about them and how the antidepressant will work in your case. It is important to know that the antidepressants do **not work instantly** and may take two or more weeks to take effect. It is equally important to know that you may not get a result at all and may need to change the antidepressant. Also, the antidepressant may work minimally, requiring further work from you.

I suppose what I am saying is *don't depend* on the antidepressant for a solution. Yes, it may help, but in my experience, *changing the quality of my thinking* also helped. This is where a psychologist or psychiatrist will help.

I have taken three different antidepressants over a period of about eight years. All three were serotonin and/or norepinephrine reuptake inhibitors, but so far, they have worked minimally. This suggests to me that I might need a monoamine oxidizer inhibitor (MAOI) as an alternative depressant, but these work differently and may produce complications, such as stroke or high blood pressure if I don't follow a diet strictly. An MAOI has not been offered to me as an alternative, possibly because of the complications it *may* cause. I will be guided by my doctor.

Now, we know that monoamine oxidase (MAO) *breaks down* the neurotransmitters, which may possibly lead to depression, but it also has another function. It also controls the level of tyramine, an amine that is *responsible* for blood pressure. If the function of MAO is inhibited, then the levels of tyramine may increase, resulting in increased blood pressure, possibly leading to hypertension and stroke. Many foods also have tyramine, hence the need to be on a strict diet if prescribed MAOIs to reduce depression. If you are willing to stick with the diet and to work with your doctor, then this antidepressant may be the way to go. Again, *be guided by your doctor.*

The MAOIs also work on levels of epinephrine, which can lead to stress, since epinephrine is involved in the stress reaction. Repeated stress can also lead to depression. I won't explain the mechanism. It is sufficient to say that it involves part of the limbic system, but if relief is not found for the stress, or if the stress reaction continues due to other causes, depression may result.

So you see that depression is not a simple malady. It involves numerous sections of the brain and may even involve other regions of the body, particularly if those regions of the body are *under stress due to an accident or an operation.* So hospitalization, for instance, because of an operation, may lead to depression.

Treating the depression is important. I believe, like many of our medical authorities, that taking the medication is important as the initial step. The medication addressed the problem of neurotransmitter imbalance, where, once the balance problem has been addressed, then a psychologist can work with the individual to consider the root cause of the problem.

Remember, I became seriously depressed when I came off the medication. I thought that nothing was happening. I was waiting for the magic moment when I would be better. But hey, the medication was in fact the initial step towards improvement. I had to change my thinking to achieve the magic moment.

Classifying Depression

Depression has been classified using a variety of mechanisms. The classification used here was presented by Robert Sternberg, and for me, is simple to understand.

Endogenous (reactive) Depression. How a person reacts to the external environment. May be short term or long term. Generally is a result of what you think about the environmental influencing factor (e.g., a fight with a friend).

Endogenous (Physiological) Depression. Due to internal influences, such as an imbalance in the amount of neurotransmitters, size of components of limbic system, and possible synaptic problems in the brain. The environment is not a considered factor and may include family history for depression.

Primary Depression. Where depression *is* the main medical problem (e.g., loss of job resulting in a pervasive mood, unable to get out of bed).

Secondary Depression. Caused by another condition, such as hospitalization because of injury, or an operation. If the stay in hospital or inability to be physical is prolonged, depression may result.

Involutional Depression. Age related. Could be due to a multitude of factors, such as not being able to do the work that used to be done or no interests after work.

Postpartum Depression. Occurs after childbirth. May be short or long term, depending on circumstances. Hormonal changes usually result in short-term depression, but stress, changes in neurotransmission levels, or perceived lack of control or support may result in long-term depression.

Seasonal Affective Disorder (SAD). Usually occurs in winter because of the lower levels of light. It is possible that an individual working in an environment with low levels of light may also suffer from this condition if the low levels are consistent.

What has been called a *major depressive disorder* will fit into this classification since its main criteria is concerned with duration, not cause.

Bipolar Disorder

People who suffer from bipolar disorder suffer at both ends of the depression spectrum. They experience mood swings. We have discussed depression and what it entails. This is one end of the bipolar disorder. The other component is mania, and unlike a normal mood swing, a manic experience is heightened, just as the depression is heightened.

Some of the symptoms of mania are: irritability, positive mood, high levels of energy, easily distracted, low attention span, inappropriate behaviour, mystic experiences, and creativity. Now we may each feel these at a normal level because of a certain situation that excites us, but a person with bipolar disorder experiences them at a heightened level, often resulting in hallucinations and impaired judgment or even hospitalization.

Like depression, the causes may be varied. For instance, it may be hereditary, and evidence shows that, like depression, identical twins are more likely that non-identical twins to *both* suffer from bipolar disorder. There is evidence that high levels of cortisol, a stress hormone, can cause the disorder as can high levels of dopamine in the brain. Excess calcium levels in the brain have been linked to bipolar disorder.

It has been suggested that because some people with this disorder are creative that many creative people do, in fact, suffer from the disorder. The famous artist Vincent Van Gogh suffered from this disorder. It has also been said that a person with bipolar disorder is more likely to attempt suicide than a person suffering major depression. This may be because a bipolar person may move rapidly between the manic state to depressed state. Imagine moving from a high sense of self, and what one believes can be achieved to a level where one feels inadequate.

Like depression, there is still a lot of uncertainty about the *actual* cause of the disorder for an individual, so more often than not, the patient moves between prescribed medications until one is found that *minimizes* the symptoms.

Doctor or Psychologist?

My advice on whether you see a doctor or psychologist is to see both. I believe that one's thinking may be the primary reason why depression is ongoing for an individual, yet again, if the depression is caused by an imbalance of, say, serotonin, then antidepressants may be helpful. Having said this, it is likely that the depression, if chronic, will have a transmitter imbalance and as a consequence, or habit of thinking, the individual might dwell on the negative, thus reinforcing the depression.

I have been suffering from depression for a long time, though it became elevated after my operation. Depression is debilitating. I suffered from the "can't be bothereds," which may have cost me a promotion. I sighed a lot, became solitary for large periods of time, gave hell to my students on occasion, and probably looked miserable most of the time.

I felt that if I stabbed a long needle up the back of my brain, then the pressure would be relieved. Silly? Probably, but such is the thinking of someone who is depressed. I didn't care what I said, often offending people I didn't mean to hurt, and I often felt that a good old-fashioned cry would alleviate the problem. But men don't cry, do they?

As I said earlier, I have endured three antidepressant treatments and have visited a psychologist and a psychiatrist, yet I still feel the same—at least until now. I now know that the antidepressants were working, but I also needed the intervention of a psychologist to get to the source of the problem.

I have a strong belief that what I think about an event will affect how I will feel about the event. Being a sufferer of depression, I believe that it is important for me to persist with changing my beliefs. The depression doesn't help. When you're depressed, it is easy to accept whatever your mind presents, and the unfortunate thing with depression is that *the mind will present negative images to support your belief.* It is far easier to say, "To hell with it. I'll do it another day," and yes, you feel better when you do this, but only for a short time. Instant, short-term relief is not a cure for depression.

A term used by psychologists, "learned helplessness" (mentioned earlier), suggests that we can learn to fail. I have noticed in class that there are some students who fail repeatedly. When approached, they insist that they can't learn a concept because they are no good at maths, for example. I have heard parents say, "It is not surprising that ... is poor at maths. I was never any good, and neither was his/her father."

Hey! *It's expected to fail?* But if the failing spills over to other subjects, then the student may suffer depression. Fifteen years ago when I was teaching a remedial year-ten maths class, a male student gained a pass in one of the units. He accused me of giving him a pass to con him into performing better. Need I say that he failed his next test and he said to me, "I told you so."

Constant failure affects self-esteem, which may cause depression if nothing is done about it.

Albert Ellis and Robert Harper (*A New Guide to Rational Living*), both rational emotive therapists (RET) said in 1975, "We think it highly probable that biophysical and sensorimotor techniques for affecting human emotions, unless combined with thinking desiring methods, produce limited effect. People may get help through the use of drugs or relaxation, but unless they begin to think more clearly and value their aliveness, they will tend to depress themselves again when they stop the drugs and exercise." This is where I got to. I was being medicated and practiced tai chi, but my thinking was wrong. When I stopped the medication, everything went haywire. I suffered deeply.

It has been reported that chronic or life-long (endogenous) depression is caused by trauma in childhood that includes: emotional, physical or sexual abuse; yelling or threats of abuse; neglect; criticism; divorce; inappropriate or unclear expectations; maternal separation; conflict in the family; family addiction; violence in the family *(upliftprogram.com)*. This suggests that to alleviate the problem of depression, you will need to find the primary cause of the depression, and this cannot be done alone. You will need someone trained in bringing the problem forward to identify the root cause of the depression.

So, if you are depressed, speak to your doctor. He/she may forward you on to a psychologist or psychiatrist if you ask. Trust your doctor or health provider. Remember, if you are depressed, chances are your thinking will verify your feelings and you may talk yourself out of taking any action.

Take action. Challenge your thinking. Speak with your doctor. You will be the beneficiary of your actions, and you will feel a whole lot better.

Psychological Support

I believe that this is where the relief for depression is achieved. I said earlier, see both your doctor and psychologist. The doctor will prescribe antidepressants, which will correct the neurotransmitter imbalance but not remove the depression completely. If you know why you are depressed, change your thinking, but what better way to help improve your thinking than by speaking with someone who is trained in this area?

I have no idea why I am depressed. One moment I seem to be okay, and the next, for no apparent reason, I am a miserable sod. Do you know what's funny about this? I once trained students to analyse their thinking, and it wasn't until I went to see a psychologist that I revisited the technique. I knew it worked but had forgotten all about it. The students told me that it helped them in other ways too, such as studying.

If you are a computer geek, you might have heard of the technique. It's called mind mapping. Yes, you can purchase mind-mapping programs, but it is not essential. Good old-fashioned pen and paper will do the job just as well.

Consider the model of a mind map below.

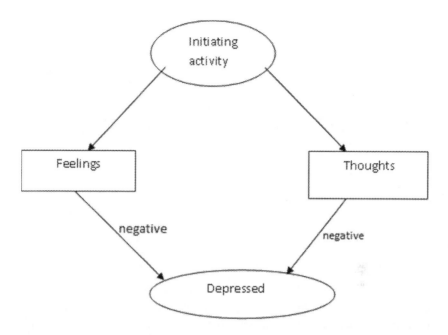

The initiating activity may be an action, thought, or feeling that leads to depression. When you draw a mind map, label the initiating activity in the circle. From this activity, we have a series of feelings and thoughts related to the event. These feelings and thoughts, if left unchallenged, may lead you to the final stage, which is the depressed feeling, the feeling you don't need to endure.

If you make a mind map, and I hope you do since it will help you overcome your problem, it is around the rectangles that you need most room since it is here that you will put words related to the feelings and thoughts.

Let me give you an example.

One day while driving my grandchildren home from school, a car passed me while driving over a speed bump. I was pissed off. What an idiot! I was already mildly depressed, and this incident made it worse. Without explaining the situation further, here is my mind map that helped reduce the level of depression.

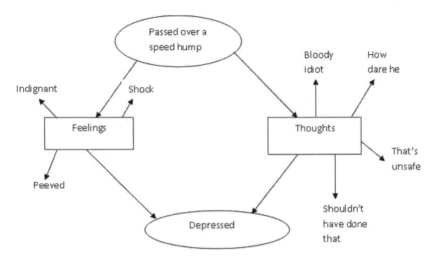

After I studied what I had written about the event, I gave thought to each word or statement. They are not written here, but I thought, *Do I need to keep dwelling on the moment?* No, of course not! In my opinion, the driver might have been a bloody idiot, but now that it was in black and white and this moment was well after the event, why dwell on it? I might have felt indignant or peeved by his silly driving, but should I let these feelings get me depressed?

It's possible that he was in a hurry to get home to his wife who was ill or expecting a baby, and I let my feelings and thoughts make me depressed for no real reason.

See how easy it is to use this map to help analyse a situation? You could add a "thoughts about my thoughts" box if you want rather than just think about it like I did. It's up to you, but whatever you do, you need to take positive action towards alleviating the problem of depression.

If your psychologist wants you to *keep a diary* of your feelings and/or thoughts, use the technique. One thing is for certain—you are not alone. You are in the hands of a trained counsellor, and if you follow his or her instructions, you will gain relief from this debilitating condition.

The psychologist I see listens to me. She takes notes and only asks questions that are relevant to what I am talking about. I can suggest anything, and she listens, occasionally negating a thought if it doesn't lead towards a solution.

I get homework on how to think and what to say when I hear someone say something that might cause me to go into a depressed state. She helps. If you think a psychologist will not help you, I urge you to reconsider. They are trained to help you to redirect your thinking; well-meaning others are not. They mean good but are using guess work, not proven techniques.

A *Spiritual* Approach

This is not an attempt to get you to attend church, but if you do go to church, use what you believe. Whether you are Buddhist, Christian, Jewish, Muslim, or some other spirituality, you can find information within your church or group to help you with depression.

Nobody likes the feeling of being depressed, particularly deep depression. It is debilitating. It is dehumanizing. It is a downer that makes you feel worthless. You don't want to go there, and if you have suffered deep, soul-destroying depression, chances are you own the mood state and possibly think that nothing can be done.

I tried a new approach (at least for me) after listening to my psychologist encouraging me to negate bad thoughts that would normally put me into a depressed state. I started to think about myself. I began to ask, "Who am I?" and "Am I the sum total of my thoughts?" Then I began to ask, "Is there something deeper within me, that truly *is* me, and therefore, I can negate the thoughts I have on the surface?"

I revisited meditation and breathing. Yes, breathing. I took long, deep, and slow breaths and expelled them slowly. At the same time, I calmed my mind and searched for answers to my questions above, often thinking more rationally about a solution. You know what? It worked!

Having just come out of a deep, depressing moment, feeling very miserable and suffering low esteem, I decided to practice what I said above since I was already depressed. I had nothing to lose. I asked, "Do I really have to feel this way?" and "Do I have to give in to my negative thoughts when depression sets in?" and "Can I stop depression before it gets a hold by stopping the thoughts?" I breathed deeply again, sat in an armchair, and took the time to think about my answers.

I didn't have to accept what my mind projected! I am not the sum of my thoughts, and I knew that I could change what was being projected to me through my mind. I even shouted at myself in my mind. I shouted, "Stop. I don't accept this" or words to that effect.

If what I have explained is not for you, if you read the Bible or Koran or any other religious book, look for inspiring statements. In fact, if you believe that God can help you, ask for that help and take action.

Give it a go. You have *nothing* to lose.

An Excursion into Naturopathy

I couldn't help myself. After I stopped taking prescribed medication and before I entered into a deep depressive episode, I went to see a naturopath who put me on a natural remedy called Adreno Tone by Metagenics. Did it work? I don't know; I still felt depressed, but I would not go back on the regular prescribed medication like Zoloft or Cymbalta. The naturopath was a learned person. I fully understood what he told me about depression, and it validated what I already knew. I had to perform a saliva test that was analysed in a laboratory. Apparently, my adrenal gland was deficient in function, which indicated that I was deficient on cortisol.

So I was prescribed Adreno Tone, which had to be taken twice daily. After three months, I felt no *apparent relief, but the level of depression did not rise.* I did, however, receive an unwelcomed side effect in irritable leg syndrome, which tended to keep me awake at night. You might be interested to know that irritable leg syndrome can be a side effect of most antidepressants. Exercise and stretching is one way to minimize the effect of this syndrome.

Again, I won't say that alternative treatments don't work. I know people who swear by alternative treatments, but I will say that the treatments did not appear to work for me, given the time span that I used them. I will say, though, that it was no worse than the doctor-prescribed medication.

It is always best to err on the side of caution and listen to your doctor. For me, I will continue to question my feelings and work at changing how I think to help minimise depression. I didn't see the point in taking antidepressants that did not work (for me). I had been taking them for many years. If the level of depression is not affected while off the medication, then why take the medication? Remember, this was my thinking *before* I went off the medication completely. I have since found out that *I need* medication to correct the neurotransmitter imbalance, and at the same time, I work on my thinking. The antidepressants set the base level of my depression. It is highly possible that Adreno Tone could have achieved the same results as my currently medically prescribed medication. I will never know.

So the levels of depression that I feel are low and still give me that "I can't be bothered' feeling. This was the level I reached on natural therapy. This suggests to me that this is my base level of depression without the intervention of psychological support. Now that I am visiting a psychologist, I will work to minimise the depression even more.

Exercise and Deep Breathing

I have already suggested that tai chi and the like may help improve the levels of depression, but these systems are not formal exercise systems. They are non-aerobic and do not add any pressure to the body. I have also found that walking and/or cycling has helped me with depression. My reasoning is that by deliberately trying to improve the state of my health, I will help myself with regards to depression.

Indeed, sites on the Internet suggest that exercise will help reduce the levels of depression. An unhealthy body with a negative mind certainly will struggle to reduce depression and more likely cause more deterioration of the sufferer's health through negative thinking and possibly increased eating.

At least it makes sense to me. Tai chi helps with one's breathing, and like meditation, when coupled with a good exercise program, will make serious inroads towards reducing your levels of depression.

If you don't like meditating, then at least take time to regulate your breathing by taking long, slow breaths in with slow expiration. Do this at least six times. It is important that you don't rush your breaths since fast breathing may produce dizziness. It has been said that the slow expiration releases hormones that help the body to relax.

Similarly, tai chi helps to relax the mind. I suppose we could say that tai chi is a moving form of meditation where you regulate your breathing while concentrating on performing the preset pattern, or form, to the best of your ability. While doing tai chi, you release all thoughts of the day, and this helps you to relax. The movements are slow and deliberate.

Now, I assume that when you hear the word meditation, you think of someone sitting cross-legged in the lotus position and repeating the sound, *"Ommmm."* Meditation doesn't have to be that!

A Simple Meditation Technique

Try this. Sit in a comfortable chair, preferably a chair where your back will remain straight. Place your feet on the floor and the palms of your hands on your thighs or the arm of the chair. Close your eyes or look down over your knee. Take a long breath in through the nose, and hold it for, say, two seconds, and then slowly let it out through the mouth. Do this about four or five times.

Now listen to the sounds around you. Try to dismiss any thoughts, or at the least, do not dwell on them; let them go. Continue to breathe slowly in and out. Do not rush it. If you need to take an extra breath, take it, and then return to a slow, rhythmical pace.

Think about your hands. Feel the pressure of your thighs on your hands, and feel the warmth. Move your mind around your body to your feet, legs, arms, chest, neck, and head. How do they feel? Concentrate on each region of the body for a minute or so. There is no need to time it; guess.

Think of a happy place, somewhere that you enjoy with your family or alone. See yourself in that place, and dwell there for about five minutes. Don't forget to breathe! Keep it slow and rhythmical. Whenever you want to come out of the meditation, return to the room and slowly look around you. Now, if you have read this instruction and have given it a go, don't you feel better?

Meditation is a way of releasing tension. Even if all you do is relax your body and breathe, you will get some benefit. The meditation is a mechanism you can use to explore your feelings. Use the technique regularly, but not if it is seen as an inconvenience.

Have you tried it? Why not! It cost you nothing but time.

Never dwell on the negatives in your life while deep breathing. You will only reinforce your negative beliefs, which may possibly send you spiralling into the pits of despair. Concentrate on the positive things in your life. Concentrate on what you can change to improve the quality of your life. I suppose what I am asking you to do if you suffer from depression is change your life for the better. Get rid of the negative aspects. You can do without it, and you can improve the quality of your thinking. It may not be instant, but you can change, and why not? Do you want to keep the negatives in your life?

Every day, take time to breathe deeply, and notice the change wash over your body. Make your deep breathing time "you" time.

In addition, walk for at least five kilometres (three miles), regulate the speed, and gradually increase the distance. Improve your breathing by following the suggestion above. Clear your mind and gain body health. You have everything to gain.

If You Do Nothing

Consider for a moment that you may be depressed. What could happen if you don't do anything about it? Yes, you might live for a long time, but the quality of life would have been eroded. You may yell frequently at members of your family, wallow in self-pity, and in general feel seriously pissed. Is it worth it?

Alternatively, you might consider suicide. This is not a stupid remark; many depressed individuals take their own lives to get rid of the pain that goes with depression. Sporting people have also been guilty of this, and sports people are physically fit. You only need to take up the thought, *I would be better off dead. No one will miss me,* and the seed is planted. But if you spoke to a health professional, a far better outcome might be plotted for you. *Nobody need die from depression.* You are needed by your family, so why put them through the pain of a premature death?

If you don't do anything, at the very least you will continue to feel depressed. However, the inaction may lead to *higher levels* of depression because of your thoughts or possibly an increased imbalance of the neurotransmitters. Yes, you may have avoided telling others that you are depressed, but how will you feel? Is it worth it?

Ron D Suffered Deeply

I met Ron recently in a local shopping plaza and he reminded me of our previous meeting when he was hospitalised. We hadn't talked about depression prior to that meeting, even though both of us were suffers. Ron had taken an overdose of medication, hoping to end his life and the suffering he experienced from this insidious disease.

I write about our meeting now, because what happened to Ron can easily happen to anyone. Ron was not weak, silly or any other description you might want to offer since I am sure that he used these descriptions of himself also. He suffered as I did from a very deep bout of depression where all thinking is highly irrational, and all self thoughts, negative.

Ron has a very functional family. He and his wife have a strong relationship and he is close to his children, yet he behaved irrationally due to his depression. He is an artist and has exhibited his work publically, even being highlighted in the local newspaper. Yet, Ron took a chair and piece of wood to his own work, destroying some of his paintings. He threw the chair at a painting, which caused his wife to seek help. It was found to be very difficult to calm him down given the state of his mind, and Ron decided to 'stuff them all' by taking an over dose.

Here was a good family man with lots of support and love, thinking of taking his own life and taking action on that thought, albeit and thankfully; unsuccessfully.

When I met Ron after his attempt on his life, he was recuperating in a psych ward. He was positive and didn't hold back on his description of what he had done.

Why is this story important to you? Here, in this short book, you have two accounts of two normal family men, wanting to take their life. Neither of us were strong drinkers, nor were we on drugs. We certainly didn't want to suffer from depression yet, well, you know the rest. We weren't immune from depression *and neither are you.* We didn't want to talk about it but, for the sake of those suffering in silence, we have opened up and told our story.

Both Ron and I hope that you learn from our experiences, and seek help, or at the very least, talk to someone about your depression. You will be glad that you did.

Support Groups

With regards to *depression*, I am open about it to everyone. I visit a psychiatrist and psychologist regularly, and the open dialog helps me to minimise this debilitating condition.

You don't have to suffer alone. Call a help line, speak to your partner and family about your feelings, and go to a website to seek additional support. Beyond Blue, www.beyondblue.org.au, is an excellent site, and it provides you with the opportunity to seek a professional who may help you. If you have made up your mind to get help, why not call Beyond Blue at 1300 22 4636? You can't lose, and you will see that support is closer than you think. The Beyond Blue website has a range of interesting information sheets that will explain the condition. Why not give it a try?

If you ignore the depression and don't talk about it, it might cause problems within the family or at work. Your family and colleagues might develop an *inaccurate opinion* about your behaviour, and this can destroy a relationship. Speak honestly about it. Talk about your depression, and talk about your feelings. Breathe. Seek help through support groups and help lines. You will feel a whole lot better for it.

Similarly, for *cancer of the prostate,* there are support groups out there, and they are very helpful. You can talk about your problem or just listen to others in the group talk about their experiences. You will be surprised at the level of support you will gain from the group, and you will be surprised at how positive the men are who have the cancer and are dealing with it daily.

Rob Tonge (Maroochydore Prostate Cancer Support Group) said, "I think what happens when men walk into a support group meeting for the first time, is that they suddenly realize they're not alone" (*Directions*, issue 2). Search for a group that meets your needs. I say this because the first group you attend may not suit you, leaving you disheartened. There will be a group that will support you in the manner you expect, so give it a go.

How do you find a support group for prostate cancer? Try calling the Prostate Cancer Foundation of Australia (PCFA) on 1800 22 0099, or a similar group in your country of origin. You could also visit the numerous cancer sites on the web, particularly www.pcfa.org.au or the Cancer Council of Australia at www.cancer.org.au. There is always Mensline Australia on 1300 78 9978 or www.menslineaus.org.au.

You have nothing to lose but everything to gain by seeking help and support from these and other organizations, so why don't you give one of them a call?

Concluding Remark

Like cancer or any other disease, depression is unwelcomed and can be taxing on the brain. We never ask to get ill, yet many of us do and will get ill in the future. If you are suffering from depression, see your doctor. Men do and will continue to get ill; that is a given. Illnesses are a fact of life, and no amount of bravado will prevent the disease from occurring.

I am certainly glad that I sought help on both fronts, the cancer and depression. I am still alive, and even though I get depressed, I know that I am normal and I can do something to help me with the situation. There are no magic pills for depression, and yes, *what didn't work for me may work fine for you.*

I have revisited tai chi and other relaxation mechanisms and am having success in reducing my depression. You can consider this too. Tai chi classes are in most suburbs, or maybe try yoga. Change your thinking. Don't fall into the trap of letting your current thoughts guide the outcome because, more likely than not, if you are depressed, your thinking will keep you in that state.

Don't suffer the consequences of masochism or bravado. Your family needs you, and you have a life to live, so live it fully and not under a cloud.

Good luck with whichever treatment lies ahead of you, and talk to you partner about your feelings. You will be surprised at the level of compassion and support you will receive. Live a long and happy life.

My email address is newbegii@gmail.com.

I have designed a *questionnaire* about *cancer of the prostate*, and if you would like to participate in a survey on this disease, email me at the above address and I will send you a *Word*-based document, which is the questionnaire. You can answer it on your computer and email it back to me. Your support will help me to help others who are currently looking into this disease, and the information supplied will be held in confidence.

What follows now is a short story that demonstrates how a person suffering from depression thinks and behaves. I hope you enjoy it. The story is fictional, as are the characters in the story. I have used my own experiences to generate the thoughts and feelings that such a depressed person may endure.

I'm too Old for This

Gary Todd, a retired secondary school teacher, works as an emergency teacher to help support his retirement fund. He decided to accept work from only two schools, both which he knew very well, and he had a deep respect for the staff at these schools.

"The students think I'm not qualified," he told a staff member over lunch. "A boy asked if I was a real teacher or just a teacher's aide. God, now I know how an ET feels when they go to class. The job's just a babysitting job, and the students think they can get away with murder."

"But you used to work here," James, an old colleague, said.

"Yeah, but that was five years ago. Most kids don't know me," Gary replied. "I'm on top of them, though. They won't get away with too much, believe me."

"I've gotta ask, Gary. Do you still suffer from depression?" James said concernedly. "I mean, if a kid decides that he is going to test you, it could trigger it."

"Yeah, I know. But you know what? Since I have retired, it feels like a big burden has been taken from my shoulders. I feel a lot more relaxed. If a kid doesn't want to work, why should I worry? Yes, I'll try to encourage him to work, but I'm not going to lose any sleep over it."

"Good for you. What class do you have next?"

"Bloody art. Geez, I wish the daily organizer would give me more of what I'm trained for, English. I don't know anything about art."

"Don't worry, Gary, the students will know what they're doing. Walk around and look official, and then sit down and read."

"Good idea, mate. As long as they are doing something, it should be okay. I just feel a little anxious at the moment, that's all."

The recess break soon ended, and Gary walked off to class, along with the rest of the staff, catching up with the latest gossip along the way.

"Have we got you today, sir?" a male student asked as Gary unlocked the door to allow the students to enter.

"We've got the old guy. He's good," the male student said to one of his class friends.

Gary smiled to himself and walked to the teacher's desk to get organized for the lesson. He turned and looked at the class; two students were play fighting to gain his attention. *Bloody hell,* he thought to himself and then said, "Okay, everyone. Take a seat and I'll read was has been planned for the day."

"What's your name, sir?" a female student asked.

"I am Mr. Todd. I used to work at this school, so I know its rules. Anyone not following my direction will be sent to the coordinator. Now let's mark the roll, and then I'll explain the lesson."

Once these two tasks were completed, he looked around to find the student he had been warned about and then helped the students get the equipment needed for the lesson. When he saw that the students were working, he walked around the class to see where they were up to within the program. "Jackson's throwing paper sir," a female student said, picking up the paper to throw back.

"Don't throw it. Put the paper in the bin," Gary told the student.

"But he threw it at me," she remarked.

"And if you throw it back, he'll only do it again."

The girl understood what Gary had implied, so she put the paper in the bin. Another sheet of screwed-up paper was thrown across the room, hitting a male student on the head. The male student immediately threw the paper back, followed by a pencil and an eraser.

"Jackson, either you stop throwing paper or you go to the coordinator," Gary said as he walked over to the offending student.

"Peter threw a pencil and rubber at me," he said. "Send him to the coordinator," Jackson replied, picking up the pencil to return to Peter as a missile.

So that's Peter Henderson, Gary thought. "Okay, class, can I have your attention, please," he said out loud.

The class quickly became quiet, and Gary said, "I have told Jackson that he will go to the coordinator if he throws anymore paper. In fact, if one more student throws paper, or anything else, he or she will accompany him. Now, please get back to your work. It's due in next lesson."

Gary walked over to Peter and said, "Peter, if anyone else does anything to you, can you try and not react?"

"Jackson and his mates are always teasing Peter, sir. They try to get him into trouble," the student sitting next to Peter said.

"Then all the better not to react, don't you think? Show me what you've done, Peter," Gary asked, turning to look at Peter's work. He assessed that Peter was no artist and suggested to him what he might be able to finish before class ended. Peter sat at his work and began to draw.

For the next fifteen minutes, Gary checked the students' work when he saw Peter reach out to a student and hit him on the back. "Send Peter to the coordinator, sir," Jackson shouted.

"Why did you hit that boy, Peter?" Gary asked after checking on the boy before sending him back to his place.

"He called me a loser and a moron," Peter replied.

"Peter, the boy got the reaction he wanted. I thought you weren't going to react. Why not tell me and get them into trouble?" Gary asked, feeling concerned for Peter and his behaviour.

The class didn't take any notice of what was being exchanged between Gary and Peter, so Gary decided to leave the situation as it was. He continued to walk around the room when Jackson got up from his seat, walked over to Peter's desk, and pushed his drawing equipment onto the floor.

"Jackson. Back to your seat," Gary shouted. Jackson walked back to his seat with his hands above his head, to shouts and clapping from his friends.

When Jackson was back behind his desk, and after he had seen that Peter was not going to retaliate, Gary walked over to Jackson and said, "You can go to the coordinator now. I will speak to him before the end of the day. Now go."

"Oh, sorry sir. Just one more chance. I promise not to do anything stupid," Jackson pleaded.

Gary softened his mood a little and reached out to grab the boy's hair. "If you do act up, I'll pull your hair out by the roots. No more silly business, okay?" he said with a hint of laughter in his voice before rubbing Jackson's head.

"Ow, you can't do that!" Jackson replied. "I'm gonna report you. You're not allowed to touch the students."

"Report me, because I certainly will tell someone. But I didn't grab hard. Surely you know I was joking," Gary said to Jackson, who was rubbing his head with his hand.

"Yeah, all right, but you can't send me to the coordinator then," he bargained.

"Jackson, I will tell the principal that I touched your head, and if you act up again in this class, you will be going to the coordinator."

Ten minutes before the end of class, while the students were packing away the equipment, Jackson flicked a brush full of paint at Peter. "That's it. Go now, thank you, Jackson," Gary said. "I'll check up on you, so don't delay."

A bell rang to signal the end of the lesson, and a rather upset Mr. Todd walked towards the administration building to report what had transpired during the class and to see whether Jackson had gone to the year-level coordinator's office. He hadn't, so he relayed to the coordinator what Jackson had done during the period.

At the end of the day, Gary went to speak with the principal about the class, particularly about his pulling of Jackson's hair. "I thank you for telling me, Gary, but you know as well as anyone else you cannot touch the students, whether it was a joke or not."

"I'm sorry, Trevor. It won't happen again, I assure you," Gary answered. When he left the principal's office to drive home, Gary felt flustered and admonished himself for touching the student. "You silly prick. Shit, what if the kid tells his parents and they want to take the incident further?" With this line of thinking now established, he became depressed. By the time he had arrived home, he was beginning to sink into a low feeling of self-deprecation.

"How was your day?" Marlene, his wife, asked when he entered the house.

Gary explained what had happened during the art period, ignoring the good classes he had during other times of the day.

"You shouldn't have touched him, Gary. What if he tries to make it bigger than it really was? You might have told the student it was a joke, but you can't trust them. Why did you do it?" Marlene asked.

"Don't know," Gary replied sulkily, feeling that he wouldn't get any support from his wife and that the incident wasn't finished with yet.

"You can talk to me. Why did you pull his hair?" Marlene asked once more.

Gary sighed and then went to the bedroom to change his clothes. He didn't want to talk about the incident anymore. Fortunately for him, Marlene had detected that he was in no fit state to answer her question, so she let it go. The remainder of the evening, including dinner, proceeded in quiet.

Sleep didn't come easily for Gary that night. He tossed and turned in the bed, and when he rose the next morning, his mood was still sour. Fortunately, he didn't have any emergency teaching work to pursue, so he moped around the house, avoiding his wife so she couldn't continue asking questions about the issue.

"I'm going to visit Gail and Brian. Do you want to come? The break might do you some good," Marlene asked.

"No thanks, love, I want to cut the grass today. It looks like rain tomorrow."

At about mid-day, the telephone rang. It was the principal of the school he had worked at the previous day. "Gary? Can you come into school? Jackson Wyatt's parents have complained about the hair-pulling incident. They threaten to take it further, but I think we could convince them not to be so rash," the principal said calmly.

"Yeah, all right. I hope this thing doesn't go any further."

Gary's mood state changed instantly. Thoughts of police involvement filled his mind, and he began to speculate about what the boy might have told his parents. By the time he arrived at the school, he was feeling very anxious and felt as if the weight of the world was on his shoulders. He rubbed his neck and rotated his head from side to side to gain some relief from the depression he felt.

"Hi, Gary, the principal will see you in a moment. He's with Jackson's parents. Can I get you a drink while you wait?" the principal's secretary said when Gary approached her.

"No thank you, Laura. I'll wait outside."

At that moment, the principal opened the door to his office and said, "Thanks for coming, Gary. Come in, and we'll clear up this problem." Then quietly, he added, "The parents are a little quieter now."

Gary smiled, shook the principal's hand, and followed him into the office.

"Mr. Todd, this is Mr. and Mrs. Wyatt, Jackson's parents. I have explained to them that Jackson was not doing what you had asked him and you touched his hair in jest," the principal explained, offering Gary a chair.

"Touched his hair! He bloody well pulled it, and there is a hole where some of the hair came out," Mr. Wyatt said emphatically.

"Now that's not true. I grabbed his hair from behind and certainly did not pull it that hard—just to make a point, that's all," Gary said, correcting the anomaly in Mr. Wyatt's explanation.

"Shit! I'd hate to see what you would do if the boy was doing something tragic. You shouldn't have pulled it at all. You have no right to touch my son."

"I know that, and I apologize for what I have done. I apologized to Jackson too."

"He's got a headache now and may be off school for a few days. What do you say to that?" Mrs. Wyatt remarked.

"He didn't have a headache in class. In fact, he flicked paint at a boy, and I sent him to the coordinator's office. I believe he didn't go and see the coordinator."

"Are you calling my son a liar? Listen, sport, I'm taking this to the police. Who do you think you are? Jackson said that that bloody Peter, the class clown, threw a jar of paint at him and you did nothing," Mr. Wyatt said angrily.

"I'm sorry to have to tell you, Mr. Wyatt, that Peter did not throw anything at Jackson. In fact, Jackson went out of his way to flick the paint at Peter. Jackson was throwing paper around the class, speaking unnecessarily, and was warned more than once about his behaviour," Gary explained as calmly as he could.

"So why are you in charge of a class if you can't bloody control the students? And are you still calling my son a liar? No wonder you're a bloody emergency teacher. You couldn't get a full-time job," Mr. Wyatt argued.

Gary was angry at this reply. He could see that no matter what he said, Jackson's parents would not listen to reason.

"Wait, Mr. Wyatt, that is not fair. Mr. Todd used to work at this school, and he has only just retired from teaching. You have no right to attack him like that," the principal remarked forcibly.

"We'll see about that! See you in court," Mr. Wyatt said as he and his wife got up from their chair to leave the office.

"Shit! That went well," Gary said sarcastically. "Now they're going to involve the police."

"I'm sorry, Gary, but we will support you. You know you shouldn't have touched the student, but I know that it was in jest, and I'll get some support from the students in the class. I'll certainly speak to Peter Henderson. I'm sure he'll verify what happened."

"Thanks, Trevor. I'll write a report and email it to you," Gary said, shaking the principal's hand, preparing to go home. "My heads in a spin over what just transpired. I can't believe it!"

The two men parted company, and Gary returned home, sinking into a deep depression as he tried to justify Jackson's parents' actions. "God! The kid lied, and they believe him. They'd rather go to the police than follow up with their son. That'll help me a lot. I bet the bastards are thinking they can get money from this. Hell! They are already saying that he has hair pulled out. What a bloody lie."

He walked around the house, bewildered. His mind was racing through a range of scenarios, all negative. He saw himself selling his house to pay court costs and the family payout. "And for what! A bloody lie. The kid and his stinking family aren't even considering what it could do to me and Marlene; I bet they are thinking about what they can do with the money."

"Hello, honey. How's your day been?" Marlene said, entering the house when Gary paced the floor past the front door.

Gary looked up and said, "Don't say anything. I went back to school because that bloody kid's parents want to involve the police."

"Oh my God," Marlene replied through her hands over her mouth. "Are you all right?"

"Am I all right? Shit, Marlene, I'm going to be sued for a simple incident by greedy parents. How do you think I feel?"

"All right, love, calm down. They may not do anything."

"Yes they will. They said that they were going to the police. How do you expect me to calm down? Hell, we might lose our house. Shit! I retire after forty years of teaching, and four weeks into retirement, I get sued. Welcome to retirement!"

"Don't be so melodramatic, Gary. Let's wait and see what happens, okay? Don't be so negative about everything."

"So I'm negative now? Thanks for the support," he replied as he walked out of the house to enter the garage. Marlene thought that she should leave him to himself until his mood changed, so she set about preparing the evening meal.

When he entered the garage, Gary broke down and cried. "Shit! I can't even retire comfortably." He tried to regain his composure, after which he thought, *Those bastards are not going to get a bloody cent from me.* His breathing was heavy, and he felt a dull pain in his chest and throat. His head seemed to be swimming in a sea of confusion as he tried to gather his thoughts. The back of his neck felt tight as he walked frantically around the garage.

He punched his chest and broke once more into a crying fit. "Why?" he cried. "What have I done to deserve this?" Once more he stopped to regain his composure. The pain in his chest was still present, but his mind was calmer. "When I take my medication tonight, I'll take a few more pills. Stuff them. I'm not letting my house go begging because of a lying, shit of a kid."

This line of thinking calmed him considerably. He had made a decision, and nobody was going to get him to change his plans. He took a deep breath and returned to the house and his wife.

"Feeling better now, love?" Marlene said when Gary kissed her on the cheek.

"Yeah. I thought about it a little. They won't go to the police," he answered calmly, not daring to disclose the reason why he thought this would be the case.

While eating the evening meal, they spoke about anything but not about the incident in question. Gary even managed a laugh and held his wife affectionately while watching television. He kissed her tenderly on the forehead and said, "I love you, and don't you forget it."

"I know you do, love. I'm glad to see that you are handling this thing better now."

He kissed her again but did not reply to her comment. His decision was made, and he was comfortable with it.

The next morning, Gary rose from his sleep feeling the best he had ever felt. His resolve was as strong as the previous night, so he went into the bathroom to take a shower but not before taking his medication. His heart beat a little faster than normally, but it didn't affect his thinking. He took out the packet of antidepressants and read the brochure inside the pack. *Nausea, dizziness, headaches, drowsiness, fatigue,* he read. *Good, with an overdose, I should faint and never wake up,* he thought as he broke open ten compartments containing the capsules.

He held them in his hand, rolling them around then, and with much resolve, he threw them into his mouth and washed them down with water. *Well, that's it,* he thought before disrobing to take a shower. While showering, he waited, as if expecting a reaction, but he had dried himself and had eaten his breakfast before he started to feel drowsy with a slight headache.

"Are you all right, love?" Marlene asked, seeing that her husband had changed colour, his skin going white.

"I don't feel too good," he answered. "I'm going to lie down for a bit."

Marlene looked on in concern when something prompted her to check the medicine cabinet. She found the open sheet of capsules on the sink, "I only bought these yesterday," she said to herself. "Oh my God! He's taken an overdose." She hurried to the telephone and called for an ambulance and then rushed into the bedroom, where Gary lay in apparent rest. She shook him, shouting, "Wake up, Gary. Wake up. Don't go to sleep." But it was too late. Gary was in a coma, unaware of the panic and anxiety he had caused for his wife.

Marlene cried bitterly, shaking her husband and punching him on the chest. She heard the doorbell ring and hurried to open it. It was the paramedics. She quickly showed them where Gary was and rushed to the kitchen to vomit into the sink. Her breathing was erratic, but she calmed herself and took a drink of water when the telephone rang.

"Mrs. Todd? I'm Mr. Simons, principal of ..."

"Gary's in a coma, Mr. Simons. I have to go."

"Wait! Tell me which hospital, and Mrs. Todd, the parents have withdrawn their complaint."

Marlene broke down and cried. "A little, late isn't it? There wasn't anything in the whole ordeal in the first place," and she hung up the phone.

Gary had indeed overreacted. There was no need to take the pills, but his condition and current thinking caused him to react the way he did. And now his wife was affected. She cried bitterly for her husband, both for his life and over the fact that nothing was ever going to come of the incident that occurred during Gary's day of emergency teaching.